THE COTSWOLD WAY

Stanton Reservoir

THE COTSWOLD WAY

BY

KEV REYNOLDS

Photographs by the Author

CICERONE PRESS
MILNTHORPE CUMBRIA

First published 1990
Revised edition 1994

ISBN 1 85284 049 8

Cicerone Press guidebooks by the same author:
The Wealdway and The Vanguard Way
Walking in Kent
Walking in Kent - Volume II
The South Downs Way & The Downs Link
Walks & Climbs in the Pyrenees
Walks in the Engadine - Switzerland
The Valais-Switzerland
The Jura (with R.Brian Evans)
The Alpine Pass Route
Chamonix to Zermatt (The Walker's Haute Route)
The Bernese Alps
Walking in Ticino - Switzerland
Central Switzerland
Annapurna - a Trekker's Guide

Advice to Readers

Readers are advised that whilst every effort is taken by the author to ensure the accuracy of this guidebook, changes can occur which may affect the contents. It is advisable to check locally on transport, accommodation, shops etc but even rights-of-way can be altered and, more especially overseas, paths can be eradicated by landslip, forest fires or changes of ownership.

The publisher would welcome notes of any such changes

CONTENTS

ACKNOWLEDGEMENTS

A word of thanks to Derek Roberts and my wife Linda who, at different times, walked part of the Cotswold Way with me, shared many of the pleasures and in so doing added to my own enjoyment of this splendid corner of the country. I am also grateful for the warm hospitality received in bed and breakfast houses along the Way, for readiness of Cotsallers to impart knowledge and advice of a kind that only locals can, and especially to all the anonymous ramblers and volunteer wardens who, over the years, have waymarked the route so effectively and kept obstructions to a minimum. All who tackle the Cotswold Way are indebted to their enthusiasm and dedication; this guidebook is a modest thank you to each one.
Kev Reynolds

* * *

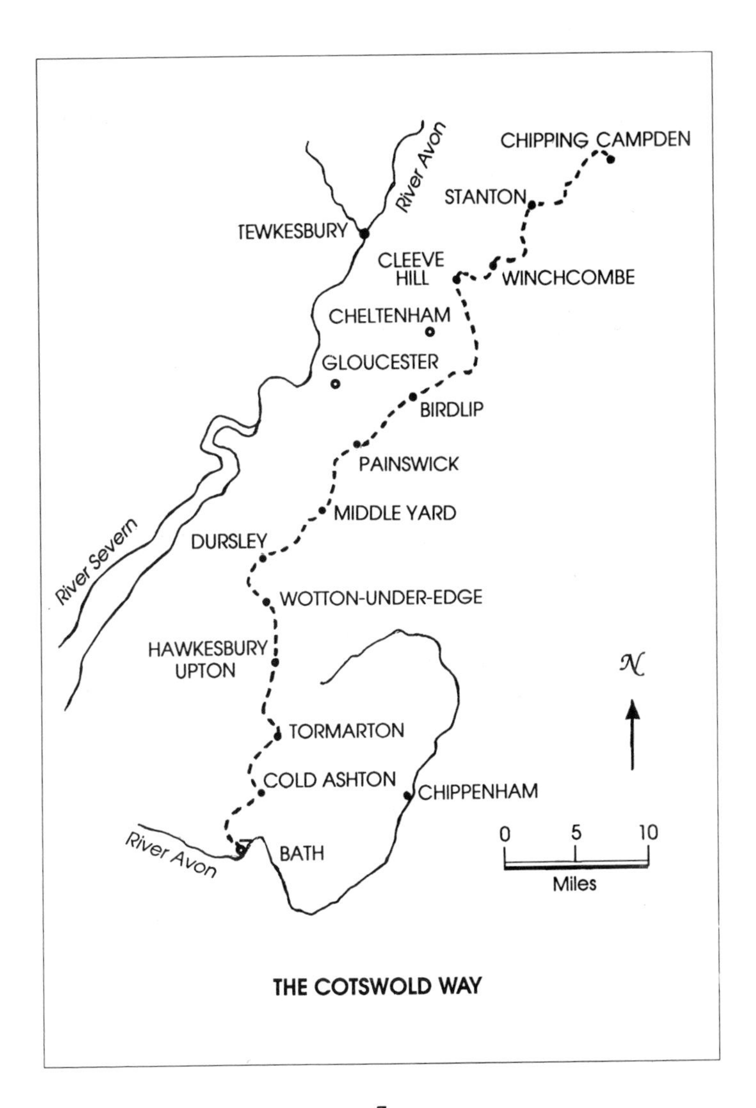

THE COTSWOLD WAY

The old market hall in Chipping Campden

INTRODUCTION

The wolds are a mellow upland feature of an extensive belt of limestone that runs from the Dorset Coast in the south to Yorkshire in the north. The highest and broadest part of that belt is an undulating tableland raised on its western side and draining gently towards the east, down to the Thames Valley and the Oxfordshire Plain; the much-loved region known as the Cotswolds. A green baize tableland it is, with jutting prows and pocket coombes, fuzzed with woodlands and chequered with drystone walls. The occasional mounds are evidence of man's long history of occupation along the very rim of the escarpment; early man used the broad views from this escarpment to warn him of approaching danger. Today the Cotswold wayfarer uses those same viewpoints as beacons of glory, highlights of the walk, places to sprawl in the grass and dream among the flowers.

From end to end the Cotswold Way weaves its devious route for 102 miles. It's a switchback, a stuttering, to-ing and fro-ing, climbing and falling walk. One moment you're wandering high along the scarp edge with toy-like farms and cottages speckling the lowland plains far below, the next you're heading down to them - down to explore a magical village or a small market town with age in its streets, charm in almost every window and the walls "faintly warm and luminous, as if they knew the trick of keeping the lost sunlight of centuries glimmering about them." Then you head up again, zig-zagging back and forth in order to capture the best the wolds can offer.

Despite its popularity the Cotswold Way has never achieved the status of an official long distance path blessed by the Countryside Commission (through which it would qualify for 100% grant aid towards improvement and maintenance), but was developed by Gloucestershire County Council as a recreational route following a suggestion made by the District Committee of the Ramblers' Association as long ago as 1953. As one of the County Council's major initiatives to mark European Conservation Year the route was eventually launched in May 1970 during National Footpath Week, and five years later its full length was treated to a concentrated effort of waymarking, mainly by volunteers from the Ramblers' Association and the Cotswold Voluntary Warden Service. It has subsequently become one of the most effectively waymarked long distance walks in Britain.

The Cotswold Way follows no historic route (as does the Ridgeway Path or the Pilgrims' Way for example), but rather it links a number of existing rights of way - footpaths, bridleways, 'green lanes' and a few short stretches of minor road. The Cotswold Warden Service undertakes a constant review of the route and embellishes it with minor alterations and improvements where necessary. This inevitably means that any guidebook may therefore be found to be incorrect in certain areas at some time in the future, but with the exemplary method of waymarking 'in the field' this should not cause too many difficulties. Simply follow the waymarked route as you find it; that will be the up-to-date Cotswold Way.

Waymarks follow the standard approved Countryside Commission method of using different coloured arrows: yellow for footpaths; blue for bridleways; white for public roads. What differentiates Cotswold Way arrows from other route directions is the white spot (about the size of a ten pence piece) painted on or by the arrowhead. Where the route goes through a town, waymarks may be seen on kerbstones, on the posts of traffic direction signs or on a wall. Where it crosses large arable fields, a sizeable target disc will sometimes be seen fixed to a tree or telegraph pole as a direction aid, and where the route crosses a golf course (on Cleeve Common and Painswick Hill, for example), low wooden waymark posts will be seen.

This is a route, like a number of others, that best repays an unhurried approach; a route with so many places of interest nearby that no walker ought to resist the temptation to stray here and there in order to broaden his overall view of the region. 'Intently haphazard' is a term which admirably suits this attitude to walking the Cotswold Way.

Chipping Campden makes a worthy beginning, Bath a worthy

end. Between the two the Way follows a meandering course through woodlands, along the western rim of the escarpment for mile after mile, down into secretive coombes, along the banks of mill-streams, over sunny belvederes, exploring one glorious village after another - always seeking to reveal the very essence of the Cotswolds, the spirit of the region. And it works. It works supremely well.

MAN IN THE LANDSCAPE

Man in the landscape could well be this walk's theme. The Cotswolds have no vast wilderness, no raw mountains or trackless moorland; it is not a countryside that threatens or bullies, but rather one that welcomes with a smile. Man has lived here in harmony with nature for a long time, using as a basic material for building the very substance of the land, creating a rare degree of artistry in the moulding of wall, doorway and crooked roof, until even the villages themselves appear as an extension of that land. Man, indeed, as part of the landscape.

Instead of shunning habitation, as do so many other long distance paths, the Cotswold Way actively seeks out the timeless villages and towns that are among the loveliest features of the region. Yet timeless though they may at first seem, these villages and towns are in truth only recent additions to a landscape that has been worked, in some form or another, for five thousand years and more.

The first Cotsallers were nomads, hunter-gatherers who drifted through what was then a heavily wooded region, but who made little visual impact on it. It was Neolithic man, around 3000 BC, who first began to clear patches in the woodland cover and to till the soil, and in so doing started a primitive form of landscape management. These groups of New Stone Age agriculturalists left behind some 85 burial tombs scattered throughout the Cotswolds, among the finest being Hetty Pegler's Tump and Belas Knap, both on or very close to the Cotswold Way. These ancient relics are distinctive of what has become known as the Severn-Cotswold Group; large cairns of stone with a covering of soil and internal passageways lined with drystone walling which open into burial chambers. It has been estimated that some of these tombs must have involved about 15,000 man hours to build, which indicates a surprising level of social involvement and organisation.

As well as Hetty Pegler's Tump and Belas Knap, there's another similar burial mound of the same period on Frocester Hill, while at Crickley Hill near Birdlip recent excavations have revealed evidence of a 3 acre Neolithic causewayed camp which contained a village protected by earthwork defences consisting of a double ditch and dry walling topped by a palisade. The discovery of flint arrowheads and items of charred fencing suggest that life in the Stone Age was not entirely peaceful.

Neolithic man was replaced by tribes of immigrants from the Low Countries. These so-called 'Beaker' people of the Bronze Age lived a mostly nomadic existence, raising stock and undertaking a primitive form of cultivation before moving on. The most significant evidence of the occupation of the Cotswolds (though they are not always clearly visible) is in the form of round barrows, by contrast to the long barrows in which their predecessors had buried their dead. Although there are more than 350 of these round barrows, none of any importance are actually to be seen along the Cotswold Way.

What is visible, however, and in dramatic form, is a series of hill and promontory forts dating from the Iron Age which lasted from about 700 BC until the Roman occupation. It is thought that these defended enclosures served different purposes. Some clearly contained working communities with villages of long houses; some were market centres or animal corrals; some of the smaller enclosures perhaps were the fortified homes of tribal chieftains of the *Dobunni*, as these Belgic immigrants were called. Yet whatever their function they conformed to set patterns, being protected by deep rock-cut ditches and tall, near-vertical walls. Nowadays they invariably appear as rounded, grass-covered mounds, some saucer-shaped and distinctive, others perhaps with sections of wall having been lost under centuries of ploughing.

The market cross, Stanton

There are many fine examples of these hill forts along the route, the largest being at Little Sodbury. Sodbury hill fort covers 11 acres, enclosed by ditches and earth ramparts; Uleybury is even larger at more than 30 acres, but is just off the route. Set on the escarpment above Dursley it had the additional protection of a 300 foot drop down the scarp face. Other hill forts may be seen along the way on Cleeve Common, Leckhampton Hill, Crickley Hill and Painswick Beacon, among others.

When the Romans came in 43 AD they adopted some of these Iron Age camps for their own use. In addition they built a fortress at Cirencester and another near Gloucester, then linked the two with the Ermin Way which is met on the Cotswold Way at Birdlip. Away from the towns - and none is greater in this part of Britain than Bath - agricultural estates were established and well-to-do citizens built villas for themselves, usually richly decorated with mosaics, on well-chosen sites that caught the sun. The Cotswold Way passes near two of these villas, one above Wadfield Farm near Winchcombe, the other at Witcombe below Cooper's Hill.

The Roman occupation of the Cotswolds ended in 410 AD with the withdrawal of the legions and the advance of the Saxons. The Dark Ages that followed are shrouded in mystery, but it is thought that these latest newcomers brought with them a way of life that was not ordered with the same degree of Roman culture and organisation. There seem to have been many tribal differences to settle. It was during this period that Arthur rose as defender of Britain. Tales of King Arthur are a muddle of historic evidence and legend, but that these were unsettled times cannot be in doubt. What seems certain is that towards the end of the 6th century a battle took place on Hinton Hill near Dyrham, between West Saxon warlords Cuthwine and Cealwin, and three kings of the Britons. The kings - Coinmail, Condidan and Farinmail - were slaughtered and the Britons pushed back to Wales and Somerset leaving the towns of Bath, Cirencester and Gloucester in Saxon hands.

The Cotswolds were then ruled by West Saxons in the south, and Mercian Saxons in the north. The Mercian capital was established at

Winchcombe where a monastery was founded. In Bath, which became an important and substantial Saxon town, King Edgar was crowned the first king of all England in 973 AD at the abbey there. The Church grew in power and by the end of the Saxon period a good proportion of the Cotswolds was actually owned by the Church. It was during this period that whole sheepskins were being exported from the Cotswolds to serve English missionaries on the Continent, an export that began as early as 700 AD.

Under Norman rule, following the invasion of 1066, the Cotswolds maintained an important position in the country, with England's capital being very briefly centred at Gloucester. A new phase of building began and evidence of it can still be seen today, particularly in the churches. Horton Court, a few yards off the route of the Cotswold Way, also dates from Norman times and is still in use. (It is now in the ownership of the National Trust.)

The Domesday Survey of 1086 showed that the region was already largely cultivated, but with woodland covering much of the western escarpment. More clearings were made during the following centuries and the open fields then turned to extensive sheep pasture. 'In Europe the best wool is English; in England the best wool is Cotswold.' This saying held true in the Norman era when sheep outnumbered people by four to one and exports of Cotswold wool increased accordingly.

The traditional animal of these vast sheepwalks was known as the Cotswold Lion, a breed of sheep "...with the whitest wool, having long necks and square bodies." These long necks were adorned with a shaggy woollen 'mane', which led to their nickname. By the Middle Ages the wolds were almost entirely given over to grazing these sheep, and the wool masters used their great wealth to build some of the grand houses and elegant churches (complete with lavish stained glass and intricate carvings) that now form such a feature of the Cotswold Way. Chipping Campden owes both its charm and its architectural splendour to the wool masters. Its church is a monument built on the proceeds of wool sales, as are those of Wotton-under-Edge and several more along the route.

The decline in the export of raw wool began in the early fifteenth century with crippling taxes. (Revenue from wool at one time accounted for more than half of England's fortune.) But this decline was partially addressed by the home manufacture of cloth, and the new masters of the Cotswolds were now mill owners and middlemen. They built fine houses for themselves in Painswick and the Stroud Valley, taking over from the sheep owners as financiers of a renewed spate of church building and creating a new middle class in the process.

In the 17th century the Civil War was fought here, as elsewhere, forcing a temporary halt in the fortunes that were being made. Along the escarpment several battle sites are passed on the Cotswold Way, among them a hilltop area called The Battlefields where the Battle of Lansdown was fought on July 5th, 1643. It is marked by a monument to Sir Bevil Granville. At the other end of the walk, Campden House, next to the lovely Chipping Campden's parish church, was taken as a garrison for Royalist troops, but when they left in 1645 they destroyed it by fire. Painswick's church still bears signs of a Civil War skirmish and one of the last of the battles was fought on the slopes of Dover's Hill.

Between 1700 and 1840 large areas of open land on the Cotswolds were enclosed by Acts of Parliament, which brought about the greatest change in the appearance of the landscape for hundreds of years. This was when drystone walls and hedges began to divide the wolds into the criss-cross patterns that look so attractive today. Large estates were planted with shelter belts for the raising of game birds, while the Cotswolds as a whole became much less dependant upon sheep and turned instead to a broader agricultural base with arable land replacing the sheepwalks of old. This is still principally the kind of landscape explored today on the route of the Cotswold Way.

THE BONES AND THE FLESH OF THE COTSWOLDS

Long, long ago, somewhere in the region of 180 million years ago, a warm, shallow sea covered the area now dressed by the Cotswolds.

Onto the bed of that sea settled the shells of tiny creatures and sediments of sand and clay. Slowly and persistently over untold millenia those sediments were compressed into the oolitic limestone that now forms the very backbone of the Cotswolds, and which has been used with such effect as masonry for the construction of countless lovely cottages, manor houses and churches, not to mention the long miles of drystone walling that are seen almost everywhere.

The mass of the Cotswolds lies at a tilt, with the sharp face of the escarpment to west and north and the limestone resting on several thicknesses of the soft Lias clays. Natural weathering processes are thus aided in their slow but steady destruction of the whole area: streams are constantly weakening the scarp slope, the clays slip and the overlying rock crumbles without its former support. Thus the scarp has become a corrugation of bays and projecting prows, rather like a coastline although without the tides of an ocean lapping at its base. Yet even without the wash of tides the scarp is being worn away and pushed farther east and south. 'Outliers' such as Cam Long Down near Dursley, Bredon Hill near Evesham and Dundry Hill to the south of Bristol, provide evidence of the past position of the Cotswold scarp and prove that the wolds formerly spread throughout the Severn Vale.

The bare bones of the Cotswolds were covered by an abundant flesh of vegetation once the last sheets of ice gave way, some 10,000 years ago. At first, no doubt, the wolds would have been colonised by deciduous woodlands, but in Neolithic times clearings were made and primitive forms of agriculture attempted on the virgin land. With successive generations the open spaces grew until, as we have already seen, by the Middle Ages the Cotswolds were one vast sheepwalk. Then the agricultural evolution exchanged pasture for arable land and, following the Enclosures, smaller fields were created. Now, it appears, the wheels of evolution on the land seem set to roll once more.

To the flower-loving wayfarer Cotswold limestone brings a rich treasury of orchid (green-winged and early purple in late April and

May, common spotted, pyramid, musk, bee and frog orchid in the full flush of summer); of harebells and cowslips in the meadows; wild garlic massed with bluebells in damp, shaded woodlands in spring, following a green carpet of dog's mercury in February.

Cleeve Common, which contains the highest land on the Cotswold Way at over 1,000 feet, is also one of the last remaining ancient grasslands where as many as 150 different species of herbs and grasses may be found. (The Nature Conservancy Council has scheduled this area as a Grade 1 Site of Special Scientific Interest in recognition of its almost unique natural heritage.)

Among the Cotswold grasslands white ox-eye daises are abundant. Bird's-foot trefoil, scabious, kidney vetch, thyme, salad burnet and hoary plantain, rockrose and knapweeds all combine to provide a tapestry of colour for the walker, while the hedgerows are often tangled with wild clematis (old man's beard), and clumps of hawthorn shower the slopes with a froth of bloom in spring.

Among the hawthorn bushes bullfinches and yellow hammers flash to and fro, alternating between thorn bush and gorse. Woodpeckers rattle the deadwoods, buzzards and kestrels hang seemingly motionless in the sky above open hill slopes, eyes alert for sign of small voles or mice far below. Pheasants will almost certainly threaten the unwary with heart failure as they practically explode from under your boots as you wander along the overgrown edge of a field, or through a woodland in autumn. Fallow deer may be seen in some of the larger woodlands and, with a short detour from the Way into Dyrham Park, a large herd can be studied at will. There are foxes and badgers, rabbits, hares and the scampering of grey squirrels in countless trees along the Way.

CARING FOR THE COTSWOLDS

In 1966 nearly 600 square miles of the Cotswolds were awarded the status of an Area of Outstanding Natural Beauty, and 2 years later a Voluntary Warden Service was established to take particular care of various aspects of the gently undulating wolds.

Wardens are recruited from all walks of life, with assorted talents and enthusiasms, but are united by a common love of the countryside. They regularly patrol sections of the Cotswold Way - as well as other popular footpaths - maintaining stiles and gates, clearing any particularly rampant growth and upgrading waymarks. Walk leaflets are produced by the Warden Service and guided rambles organised for the general public. They plant trees, lay hedges and undertake the maintenance of damaged drystone walls, as well as organising working parties to reduce problems caused by litter at overused sites. There is currently one full-time warden, and more than two hundred volunteer wardens involved in caring for the Cotswolds.

For more information about the Cotswold Voluntary Warden Service, or offers of help, write to:

The Cotswold Warden Office,
c/o County Planning Dept.,
Gloucestershire County Council,
Shire Hall,
Gloucester. GL1 2TN.

TRANSPORT AND ACCOMMODATION

Whilst it would be feasable for the Cotswold Way to be walked in dislocated day sections with the aid of private (and in some cases, public) transport, this guide has been written with the long-distance walker in mind. However, the Way is not the sole preserve of the hardened, single-minded rambler who storms through the countryside at a rate of 30 miles a day. The Cotswold Way best repays an attitude of gentle inquisitiveness, a dawdling perambulation that strays to investigate a site of interest off the route, that finds time to laze in the sun and dream with distant views. This guide is therefore broken into easy stages (the longest is 15½ miles while most are in the 6-10 mile range) that are dictated by the availability of accommodation. The more determined and energetic of walkers can obviously combine two or three stages in one.

Neither accommodation addresses nor public transport services are detailed in this book since they change from time to time. Prospective Cotswold wayfarers are directed instead to a first rate publication compiled by the Gloucestershire Area Ramblers' Association. *The Cotswold Way Handbook* is published every two years and details all available accommodation (hotels, bed & breakfast, youth hostels, campsites etc.) on or near the route. It also gives travel information (including bus and taxi operators), addresses of tourist information offices and outline details of places of interest to visit. This highly recommended publication may be purchased from:

The Ramblers' Association,
1-5 Wandsworth Road,
London. SW8 2LJ

Gloucestershire County Council produces *The Cotswold Bus and Rail Guide*, another annual publication of interest to those planning to divide the walk into a fragmented challenge.

WANDERING THE COTSWOLD WAY

This is a lowland walk; a walk for all who love a gentle series of landscapes, who cherish long views, snug villages, hills and vales, who delight in the songs of birds, the fragrance of wayside flowers, the sun on your face and the breeze in your hair; who care little about a day of non-stop rain so long as there are footpaths to walk and countryside to absorb through the soles of your feet.

This is no mountain trek, but it does have its occasional steep slope to negotiate and enough up-and-down to give a day's exercise that will make you feel well relieved to kick off your boots and put your feet up at the end of it!

How far you walk in the course of each day depends as much on your accommodation or transport needs as it does on your degree of fitness or the amount of time available. This guide divides the route into twelve individual sections, the shortest being only 6 miles, the longest 15½ Few regular walkers, I suspect, would be prepared to devote twelve days to a route only 102 miles long. The following suggestions are therefore given to enable the route to be completed in either 7 or 5 days, by combining various stages described in the main (south-bound) body of this book.

a) *A Seven Day Walk:*

Chipping Campden to Stanton	(10 Miles - as per Section 1 in the text)
Stanton to Cleeve Hill	($14^1/2$ miles - Sections 2 & 3)
Cleeve Hill to Birdlip	($15^1/2$ miles - as per Section 4 in the text)
Birdlip to Middle Yard	($16^1/2$ miles - Section 5 & 6)
Middle Yard to Wotton-under-Edge	($13^1/2$ miles - Sections 7 & 8)
Wotton to Tormarton	(16 miles - Sections 9 & 10)
Tormarton to Bath	(16 miles - Sections 11 & 12)

b) *A Five Day Walk:*

Chipping Campden to Winchcombe	(18 miles - Sections 1 & 2)
Winchcombe to Birdlip	(22 miles - Sections 3 & 4)
Birdlip to Dursley	(23 miles - Sections 5 to 7)
Dursley to Tormarton	(23 miles - Sections 8 to 10)
Tormarton to Bath	(16 miles - Sections 11 & 12)

EQUIPMENT FOR THE WALK

No specialised equipment beyond one's normal walking gear will be necessary for tackling the Cotswold Way. Ramblers will be aware of the need for comfortable, well-fitting boots or stout shoes. Some may prefer to wear trainers, but these give little support for ankles and on some of the steep scarp slopes the grass can be very greasy underfoot, especially after rain or a heavy fall of dew. In such circumstances you will need all the support you can get from your footwear. Certainly boots are preferable for the negotiation of muddy sections.

Shorts will be comfortable to wear on many stages at certain times of the year, although nettles or brambles tend in places to stray onto the pathway and leg protection will then be called for. In our unsettled climate no sensible walker will set out to tackle a long-distance route without carrying waterproofs. Overtrousers are often handy when crossing hayfields or fields of corn after rain, or early in the morning with overnight dew still fresh.

A light rucksack should be adequate for the carrying of spare clothing, waterproofs and overnight toilet items. In addition a small first aid kit should be packed, plus Ordnance Survey maps for an overview of the countryside through which the walk is leading. Whilst there are pubs (and occasionally shops) that serve food along the route (and a note is given wherever refreshments are available), it is advisable to carry a packed lunch and some liquid refreshment with you, just in case the timing of your arrival does not coincide with that of the publican's hours of opening!

USING THE GUIDE

This guidebook is written with descriptions for both south-bound and north-bound walkers. The main text travels from Chipping Campden to Bath, but the second part gives brief details for the journey north. It is to be hoped that the excellent waymarking along the route will mean that the descriptions and sketch maps included within these pages will be sufficient to meet your mile by mile requirements. However, at the head of each section a note is given with regard to the specific Ordnance Survey sheets covering the area described. The Landranger series 1:50,000 scale (1¼ inches = 1 mile) will provide an adequate overall picture of the route's progress. A grid reference is quoted here and there to enable you to locate your exact position with some ease.

Throughout the guide I have sought to give additional items of information on particularly interesting places and features seen along the way. In the text these are marked with a cross reference number and information is outlined at the end of each section corresponding with the numbers.

The route as written is as it appeared when I walked, checked and re-checked it, yet it is inevitable that changes will occur with time. Our countryside is not static, it evolves with the seasons and the years. Who can predict what natural forces might level woodlands overnight? Who can tell what the EEC will command of our farmers next? Will the Cotswolds revert to sheepwalks and the large acres of arable turn again to pastureland? Who can tell which planning application will meet with approval, thus resulting in buildings standing tomorrow where today no buildings may be seen? We cannot know, nor properly predict.

The Cotswold Way is, however, a well-established, superbly waymarked and maintained route. When changes occur one may feel confident that the enthusiasm of the Cotswold Voluntary Warden Service will meet the challenges presented, and that wayfarers can set out happy in the knowledge that the best available route will have been waymarked for their pleasure. As you walk, then, give a vote of thanks for the many hours of unpaid effort that have gone into making this stroll along the Cotswolds the delight that it most certainly is.

Notification of any major changes encountered along the way will be borne in mind for future editions of this guide. A postcard detailing these, sent to me c/o the publisher, will be gratefully received.

ALONG THE WAY

In these days of competitive and record-breaking walks there is a tendency for many to rush through the countryside with one eye on the hands of a watch, and no time for contemplation of the intricacies of the landscape or a leisurely appreciation of nature's gifts that are there for all to enjoy. There is, of course, much more to walking a long-distance path than burning the miles hour after hour. It can be (should be?) a journey of discovery, an exploration of the natural world about you. If you open your eyes, heart and mind to the splendours of that world, you'll grow richer by the day.

* * *

One of the finest rewards for the wanderer of long-distance footpaths is the kaleidascope of memories that settle in the mind at the end of a walk. In a rash of colourful images they conspire to warm the cold nights of winter and set the heart longing for a return, they rise unbidden as often in times of stress as they do in moments of relaxation. A walker's landscape is, after all, both a powerful stimulant and an inspiration. Certainly that is true of the Cotswolds where memories and dreams intertwine in a complex of pleasures on completion of the Cotswold Way.

Vignettes overlap one upon another: sunshine chasing cloud-shadows across the Vale of Evesham... the full glory of an immense panorama seen from the trig point on Haresfield Beacon... the swirl of the Severn gleaming far-off... the tower of Horton's church glimpsed through a filigree of autumn-tinged beech trees... the gentle dip and fold of grassland round Painswick Hill. I recall too the damp grey mists sweeping over Cleeve Common, blotting out the views and causing a moment's confusion... waterlogged Bath Lane where cold brown pools washed high above my boots... rain giving way to evening calm and birds flying off to roost with a song of optimism for tomorrow. (An optimism well-placed.)

I think of the honey-gold stone of Chipping Campden, its Jacobean market hall and identikit almshouses, of Broadway and Stanton (especially Stanton), the dusty-white buildings of Painswick, table tombs and manicured yews, the 40 gargoyles on Winchcombe's church, cottages neat with roses over their doors (the very stuff of nostalgia), tall-chimneyed manor houses and magnificent churches built from the proceeds of Cotswold wool.

Tracing the footprints of Iron Age man and the legions of Rome, one wanders through history... where Saxon armies did battle with the Britons of long ago... where cousin fought cousin in the Civil War on land where today only pheasants scamper with a clatter of confusion. On the raised mounds of hill forts sheep echo the cries of warriors 2,000 years dead... burial chambers raised on the escarpment hold secrets still... Roman villa mosaics mingled with the plough-turned soil an abbey ruin pitting skeletons of stone against a background of tree and hedgerow.

Finally the best and perhaps most pertinent of all the vignettes - the last few yards of the 100 mile walk when, coming through the streets of twilight, rounding a pillar, I heard a busker playing Mozart on a violin and there rose ahead the loveliest sight of all, Bath Abbey. Deep in shadow below, bright in floodlight above, it rose out of the darkness into the light as a symbol of peace and hope and beauty. Behind me stretched over 100 miles of wandering through a comfortable, friendly, scenic part of Britain, and Bath Abbey represented its completion. The Cotswold Way ended for me as memorably as it had begun. And in between? Well, in between there had been colour, history, romance, peace. An ever varying experience through an ever varying series of landscapes. A walk, it was, of considerable beauty. What more could anyone ask?

* * *

Finally, before you set out to walk the Cotswold Way, please remember the countryside needs your care and respect.

* Guard against all risk of fire.
* Fasten all gates.
* Keep all dogs under close control.
* Keep to the waymarked path across farmland.
* Use gates and stiles to cross fences, hedges and walls.
* Leave livestock, crops and machinery alone.
* Help to keep all water clean.
* Protect wildlife, plants and trees.
* Take special care on country roads.
* Make no unnecessary noise.

The Country Code quoted above follows in the wake of principles set by Octavia Hill, a champion of the countryside and one of the founders of the National Trust who wrote at the turn of the century:

> "Let the grass growing for hay be respected, let the primrose roots be left in their loveliness in the hedges, the birds unmolested and the gates shut. If those who frequented country places would consider those who live there, they would better deserve, and more often retain, the rights and privileges they enjoy."

* * *

SOUTH-BOUND ROUTE
CHIPPING CAMPDEN to BATH

INTRODUCTION

Walking south along the Cotswold Way is to make a pilgrimage with Bath, its Regency splendour and the glory of its Abbey, beckoning from afar. True you may well have the prevailing wind in your face, but this is hopefully compensated for by long views and sunshine on your brow. This route is a little less strenuous than heading north where there's rather more up than down, also - and this is important - the essential harmony of the Cotswolds is with you from the very start.

Before setting out from Chipping Campden time should be allowed for an unhurried exploration of the town. There is much to see and to admire, so much to absorb, to file away in the memory and to resurrect in other towns and villages along the way. Then almost as soon as Campden is left behind there are long views to soak in and the first of many walks along the escarpment to Broadway Tower, down to Broadway and over breezy heights again to reach Stanton and Stanway.

The escarpment is gained and lost countless times on the way to Bath, the first day or two being particularly clever at finding fresh excuses to drop to the plain and then climb up again. There are field paths, woodland trails, old drove roads and saltways, green lanes and minor roads winding between hedgerows lively with sparrows and wrens, fragrant with honeysuckle in spring and early summer, and providing wide panoramas across the plains.

From Stanway there's an up and down stretch to the ruins of Hailes Abbey and across undulating farmland to Winchcombe with its pretty cottages, village stocks and gargoyles round the church. After

Winchcombe there's Belas Knap (worth half an hour of anyone's time), then on to the highest part of the whole route on Cleeve Common.

Cleeve Common leads to Leckhampton Hill, another lofty belvedere overlooking Cheltenham, with the eye-catching digit of the Devil's Chimney jutting from a lower scarp terrace. South of Leckhampton is Crickley Hill, where history lies partially exposed beneath your boots and an observation platform provides an opportunity to look back a thousand years and more.

Between Crickley Hill and Cooper's Hill the Way crosses just below Birdlip which sits astride the Roman route of the Foss Way. Woods conceal the broadest views, but the approach to Cooper's Hill still allows plenty to gaze at, with a soft light flooding through the trees. More woods stretch along the escarpment, but you emerge onto Painswick Beacon, open and green, splashed with silver birch and birdsong. Down then to the whitest of all Cotswold towns. Painswick has a churchyard known far and wide for its table tombs and exquisite yews - but there's much more besides.

From Painswick a climb leads onto Scottsquar Hill and to what many consider the finest viewpoint of the whole walk, Haresfield Beacon. This is indeed a tremendous knoll from which to gaze out over the Vale of Gloucester, the River Severn and the Forest of Dean. After absorbing all you can from here it's into woods for the downhill stretch which takes the path into the industrial valley overlooked by Stroud.

From cloth mills on the River Frome to woodlands hanging from the steep scarp slope takes only an hour or so. Peace and serenity are restored as you regain the escarpment for huge views looking out to a pair of outliers which soon have to be crossed. Near Hetty Pegler's Tump the Cotswold Way plunges down the scarp, then climbs up and over Cam Long Down and Cam Peak before swooping down once more - this time into Dursley.

Dursley leads to Stinchcombe Hill, and then from Stinchcombe Hill to North Nibley, Nibley Knoll and Wotton-under Edge. (What names there are to conjure with in the Cotswolds!) Wotton has its mill streams, and the stage beyond Wotton explores a narrow valley lit by a lively little stream that once powered several mills. One of these is passed on the way to Hawkesbury Upton.

Out of Hawkesbury you follow Bath Lane (an ancient trading route). Horton is next, closely followed by Little Sodbury and Old Sodbury, through Dodington Park and up to Tormarton (sitting pretty on the edge of a motorway hell). Dyrham seems all but forgotten in its leafy dell; Cold Ashton smiles out to the south and as you leave it along Greenways Lane, so a luxurious bowl of countryside draws you on.

It's not far then to Bath. Over The Battlefields, along the escarpment once more, round a golf course and across an Iron Age hill fort and you come to Prospect Stile with the first view of Bath lying in its hollow. Best of all here is the view onto Kelston Round Hill, one of the finest of all the hills seen since leaving Chipping Campden. The way down leads round the shoulder of the hill and into Regency Bath, along a maze of elegant streets until at last you come face-to-face with that gem of an abbey. This sight alone is worth walking the Cotswold Way for.

* * *

SECTION 1: CHIPPING CAMPDEN to STANTON

Distance:	10 miles.
Maps:	O.S. Landranger series; Sheets 151 (Stratford-upon-Avon & Surrounding Area) and 150 (Worcester, the Malverns & Surrounding Area) 1:50,000.
Accommodation:	Chipping Campden - hotels, b&b. Broadway - hotels, b&b, camping. Stanton - b&b, camping.

The walk begins rich with promise but with a temptation to delay, for Chipping Campden is surely the loveliest of all the Cotswold market towns, full of interest and packed with architectural gems softened by a golden honey-coloured stone. This is Cotswold vernacular at its best, but within these first 10 miles there will be other places, other villages similarly destined to slow the pace and tease with delight - Broadway is one, Stanton is another.

As soon as Campden's streets are left behind, the route starts to climb onto the escarpment where Dover's Hill rewards with a long view across the Vale of Evesham to the distant Malvern Hills. Breaking away from the scarp edge the Way continues along what is known as The Mile Drive, over fields and across the A44 on Fish Hill to the base of BroadwayTower and more fine views.

Broadway, that busy, popular honey-pot of a village, lies below the tower and field paths lead directly to it thus allowing an opportunity to walk its street, sample its tea-rooms and dodge its traffic before returning to the hills again above Buckland. The continuing route takes you along the scarp edge on a clear track for a mile and a half, but on reaching Shenberrow Hill you leave the uplands once more and wander down through lush green meadows to the manicured perfection that is Stanton.

On this initial stage of the walk you will experience the very essence of the Cotswolds, the mellow glory of its buildings and the enchantment of the breezy wolds with their extensive panoramas. If by the time you reach Stanton you've not been captured by the charm of this countryside, you

The parish church of St. James, Chipping Campden
and gateway of the long-destroyed Campden House

should consider returning home at once, selling your walking boots and settling down to a lifetime of watching TV.

* * *

The official start to the walk is in Chipping Campden High Street, but it would be more satisfactory to begin at the Parish Church of St James (1), found at the north-eastern end of the town (Grid ref: 155395).

Leaving the church, and the curious gateway to the long destroyed Campden House next to it, walk along Church Street passing a row of 17th century almshouses on your right and a cart wash on the left. On reaching the High Street bear left and walk along it, pausing here and there to admire the numerous attractive features which help to make Campden such a delightful place. (See the notes at the end of this section.)

Passing Sheep Street, which breaks away to the left, continue ahead

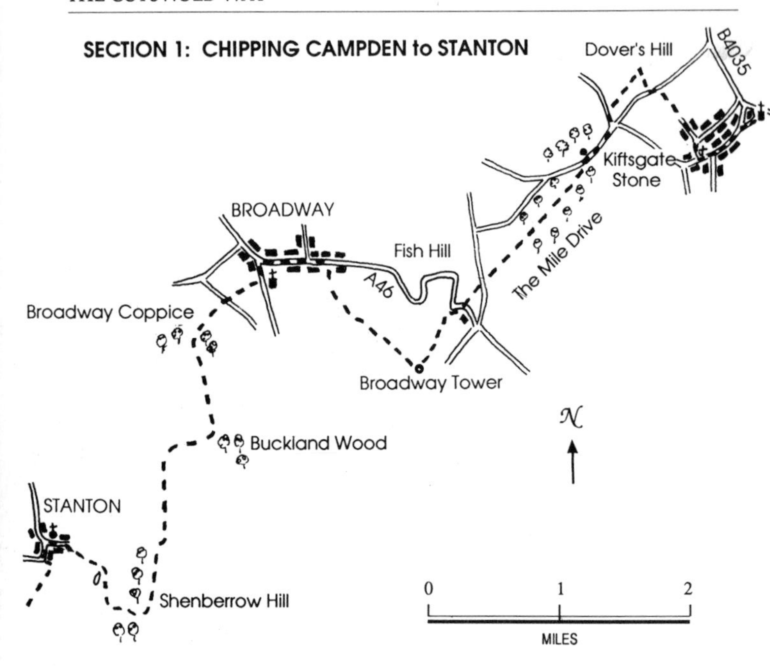

along Lower High Street, but leave this to take the first road on the right by St Catherine's Roman Catholic Church. This road soon bears right with another (Hoo Lane) branching left by a thatched cottage. Walk along Hoo Lane, which is at first residential, and when the surfaced lane ends a farm track continues ahead rising easily uphill. This is soon accompanied by a footpath which, after a short step, brings you to a country lane. Bear left along Kingcomb Lane for about 100 yards, then you will find a signpost directing you through a gap in the hedge on the right and along a footpath to Dover's Hill and Aston-sub-Edge. (Note that practically all along the Cotswold Way signposts give distances in kilometres.) The footpath follows the right-hand edge of a field, and as you progress so views begin to open ahead and half-right to the continuing Cotswold ridge with its scarp

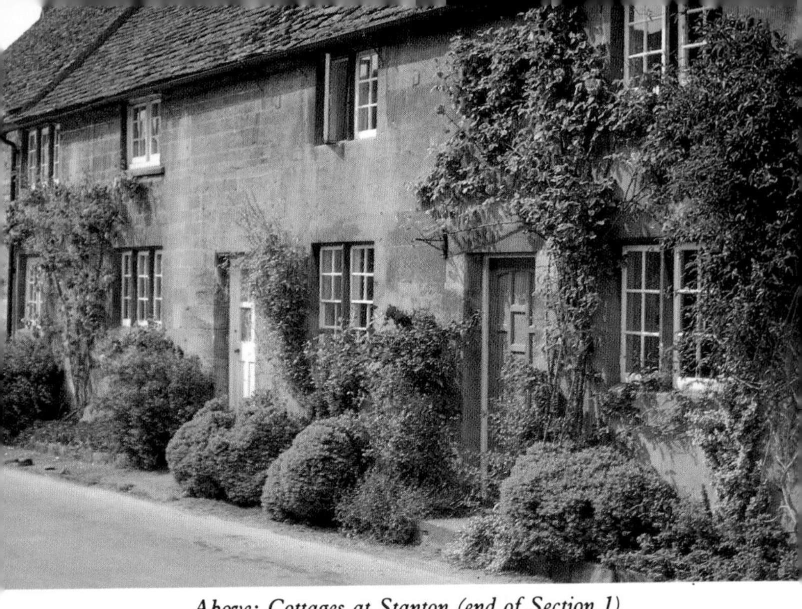

Above: Cottages at Stanton (end of Section 1)
Below: Witcombe Reservoir and Birdlip Hill, from Witcombe Woods (Section 5)

slope disappearing into the broad plain of the Vale of Evesham - a lovely, welcoming view.

At the end of the field you cross a stile and find yourself on the very edge of the escarpment; a flood of light and an extensive panorama, the first of many to enjoy along the Cotswold Way. This is Dover's Hill (2).

Turn left and walk along the narrow strip of grassland, with those big views off to your right, until you come to a long wooden fence with a field gate and memorial stone dedicated to Captain Robert Dover (1582-1652). Pass through the gate and cross the National Trust car park to a country lane where you bear left, then wander downhill to a small crossroads. Now head to the right, once again following Kingcomb Lane towards Willersey and Broadway. (Take care as you walk along this lane as traffic travels rather too fast for comfort along the straight.) Along this stretch, half-hidden by undergrowth on the right, is the Kiftsgate Stone, an ancient meeting place (3). After about 400 yards or so leave the lane by way of a stone stile on the left (next to a field gate). A few paces later bear right through a gap in a stone wall on the edge of a spinney. This brings you to The Mile Drive.

The Mile Drive is a level walk along a grassy avenue with views now to the left (south-east) into Tilbury Hollow. Half-way along you cross a farm drive and continue ahead. At the far end go through a gap in a drystone wall on the right, then half-left across a field corner to a second wall. Continue in the same direction until you come to another country lane. Over this the footpath maintains direction (sign to Broadway) and leads to a picnic area with a topograph beside the A44, opposite The Fish Inn. *(Refreshments)* (Grid ref: 119370). At this point you leave Gloucestershire and briefly enter the county of Hereford and Worcester.

The path goes parallel with the road, then crosses it to a track. After a few paces bear right on a footpath into a wood. You emerge into meadowland gruffed with curious humps and hollows, which may be explained by the fact that the site was used as an Anglo-Saxon burial ground (in 1954 a number of human bones were exposed by a mechanical digger). Soon after bear half-left through a shallow cleave with Broadway Tower seen rising ahead (4) (Grid ref: 114362). On reaching the tower go through a gate and immediately turn right.

The tower occupies a grassy knoll and gives superb views over the Vale of Evesham, with chequered fields below and the scarp edge folding away in a series of spurs and coombes as far as the eye can see.

The path descends the slope along the right-hand edge of fields towards the village of Broadway. As you come to it bear left and walk along the main street into the village proper (5) *(Refreshments, accommodation, shops)*. A handsome, much-spruced village on a wide street (hence 'broad way'), it has for all its elegance been partially betrayed by a plethora of signs and advertisements calling the visitor to come and spend. Commercialism has been let loose, and a nose-to-tail procession of motor vehicles does nothing to enhance its beauty! However, it is possible to see through the dual screens of commerce and traffic and still enjoy the very substance of what is, after all, a lovely colourful 'heart of England' village.

Keep along the main street, which is lined with red chestnut trees, heading west until you come to the village green. Turn left here into Church Street past a thatched cottage and make towards *The Crown and Trumpet* and the Parish Church of St Michael's. Soon after passing the church turn right onto a track (signposted to Buckland and Shenberrow), then go beyond a few houses into the meadowland ahead. The continuing path may be seen climbing the tree-covered hill.

When you come to a narrow crossing lane (West End on the map), you are confronted by a choice of paths. The right-hand path goes to Buckland, but directly ahead, over a stile, our path goes up to the crown of woods at the top of a meadow slope. Enter Broadway Coppice (a mixture of hazel, oak, birch and ash) where the path winds on to emerge into a hilltop field. Now bear left along the field edge, and, at the end of this, go round the back of a stable-cum-barn, then right at the end to join the main track heading left. At this point you re-enter Gloucestershire.

The farm track now takes you almost due south for nearly half a mile towards more wooded hills. At the end of the track enter an untidy farmyard area (there is no farmhouse here), bear right and follow a rough track going along the right-hand edge of a field, rising steadily and with tree-screened views soon showing into the valley off to your right and Buckland nestling at the foot of the slope.

Continue on the track, passing through a field gate with a crown of trees half-left ahead, and walk below a lovely line of beech trees to come onto the crest of a ridge. Views open once more. On the left stands a collection of derelict farm buildings. The ridge narrows considerably, green and rabbit-shorn, with grey drystone walls criss-crossing and the slopes bearing a mixture of scrub and grassland habitats. In their season cowslips and early purple orchid paint the hillside with a flush of colour. Bullfinch and yellow hammer flit to and fro and jackdaws croak from the topmost woods.

The track takes you above a region of hollows on the left (one time quarries), then goes through a metal field gate. About 100 yards later you must bear right over a cattle grid on a cart track which curves through a long meadowland, keeping near the scarp edge with the mixed woods of Long Hill Plantation on your right.

Coming to Shenberrow Hill (6) (Grid ref: 080335) you pass a farm and hill fort off to your left, go through a field gate and descend to the right through a tight cleave among trees. (This can be rather muddy in inclement weather.) At the bottom of the cleave the path forks. Bear left and follow waymarks leading down the right-hand side of meadowland, then bear right over a stile into an adjacent meadow and continue downhill towards a pond seen in a hollow. (This is Stanton Reservoir, a pleasant corner giving a dazzle of light amidst the trees.) Keep above the pond to the right, cross a stile and bear left to pass below its northern end. A track now leads down to Stanton, a glorious little village with almost-perfect cottages lining an almost-perfect street (7) *(Refreshments, accommodation, shop)* (Grid ref: 070342).

Things Seen on the Way:

(1) **Chipping Campden** sets a seal of approval on the Cotswold Way. Its elegance stems from the wool trade and there are many

buildings seen today that owe their existence directly to it. Standing side by side along both sides of the High Street are fine houses with leaded windows and splendid doorways. There are tea-rooms, shops and inns, their gables uniform, roofs steeply pitched, doorways deeply set in shadow. The open-sided Jacobean Market Hall is an eye-catching feature. It was built in 1627 by Sir Baptist Hicks, a wealthy local benefactor. Now owned by the National Trust, it once was used to shelter stallholders from all weathers. Nearby is the 14th century Woolstaplers' Hall which houses the town's museum and tourist information centre; opposite this is Grevel House, built in 1380. William Grevel, whose home it was, has Gloucestershire's largest memorial brass in the Parish Church of St James. St James' is considered one of the best examples of a Cotswold 'wool' church. Parts of the south wall are 13th century, but the majority belongs to the 15th. It is reached along an avenue of twelve lime trees planted in 1770 to recall the twelve apostles. There is much within to study and admire. Next to the church are the fanciful gateway and onion-topped lodges that mark the entrance to one time Campden House, also built by Sir Baptist Hicks at an unbelievable cost of £29,000 in 1615. 30 years later it was burned down by Royalist troops in the Civil War. Alongside Church Street on a raised pavement stands the row of almshouses built in uniform loveliness during the reign of James I, once again by Hicks, to house twelve of the local poor at a cost of £1,000. The Campden Trust, founded in 1929, works to preserve the very best of this splendid old market town. *(Tourist Information Office (April-Sept): Woolstaplers' Hall Museum, High Street, Chipping Campden. Tel: Evesham 840289.)*

(2) **Dover's Hill** is named after Captain Robert Dover (1582-1652), a somewhat eccentric and wealthy lawyer who organised his first 'Olympick Games' here at Whitsuntide 1612. These games included such entertaining sports as shin-kicking, leapfrog, wrestling, skittles and singlestick fighting. Apart from an interruption during the Civil War (one of the last battles of which was fought on the slopes of Dover's Hill), the games continued annually until 1852 when they were stopped by the enclosure of the Parish of Weston-sub-Edge.

Dover's Games were revived in 1951 and now take place each Spring Bank Holiday; part of the celebrations include a torchlight procession. In the 1920's Dover's Hill was saved from development by the artist Frederick Griggs and, in 1929, the site was given into the care of the National Trust.

(3) **The Kiftsgate Stone,** found in the roadside undergrowth of Weston Park Wood half a mile south-west of Dover's Hill, marks an important Saxon meeting place (or 'moot') where representatives of surrounding districts gathered to discuss common problems and the Hundred Court convened to make proclamations and, perhaps, to administer justice.

(4) **Broadway Tower** is a prominent landmark occupying a site on the scarp edge at 1,024 feet above sea level. Designed by James Wyatt for the sixth Earl of Coventry in 1798, it is a Norman-style keep 55 feet high, a folly with three rounded turrets from which, it is said, the panoramic view encompasses a dozen counties. A telescope at the top of the tower enables the visitor to see the Welsh mountains, as well as Warwick Castle and Tewkesbury Abbey. Even without paying an entrance fee and climbing to the top, the view from the base of the tower is extensive. The countryside around the tower is now part of Broadway Tower Country Park. The Tower Barn is about 150 years old, and Rookery Barn houses an information centre.

(5) **Broadway,** it is said, was discovered by William Morris, and in his wake came a number of artists over the years. It is easy to understand its attraction, for the village is indisputably one of the loveliest of all those that line the foot of the wolds. There are two churches: the older, St Eadburgh's, which dates from the 12th century is about a mile to the south on the Snowshill road; the other church, the Victorian St Michael's, stands on the route of the Cotswold Way near The Crown and Trumpet. Half-hidden by a yew hedge nearby is the Abbot's Grange, dating from about 1320. The 'broad way' of the main street is lined with an avenue of red chestnut trees and soft Cotswold stone frontages. The village is very old and developed as an important staging post in the coaching era, (it is on the main route from Oxford to Worcester). Horses were changed here for the steep

Broadway Tower

haul up Fish Hill. Nowadays horses have been exchanged for horse-power and Broadway is a snarl of traffic and a clutter of commerce. Yet through it all the village's basic charm shines clearly. *(Tourist Information Office: Cotswold Court, The Green, Broadway. Tel: 853431.)*

(6) **Shenberrow Hill** above Stanton is the site of an Iron Age hill fort of about 2½ acres or so. In 1935 the site was excavated and various artefacts revealed, among them pieces of pottery, a bronze bracelet and two bone needles.

(7) **Stanton** has been called the 'perfect' Cotswold village, and not without good reason. It is, in truth, almost too perfect, like a Hollywood director's idea of a 'quaint' English village. In these days of bland architecture, insensitive development and myopic planning, Stanton very nearly jarrs with a sense of unreality! It's origins are simple. The village was basically a group of 16th century cottages and farmhouses (Stanton, or Stan Tun, means 'stony farm') put together with local stone in such a sympathetic manner that they seem to have grown straight out of the ground. When Sir Philip Stott came to Stanton Court in 1906 he found the village rather neglected, and from then until his death in 1937 he spent much money and architectural talent on restoring it to the splendour we see today. Unlike Broadway, Stanton has not been over-run by the motor car, or by advertisements. As such one wanders through in a dream of past centuries.

* * *

SECTION 2: STANTON TO WINCHCOMBE

Distance:	8 miles.
Map:	O.S. Landranger series; Sheet 150 (Worcester, The Malverns & Surrounding Area), 1:50,000.
Accommodation:	Stanway - b&b, camping. Winchcombe - b&b.

A series of field paths lead the continuing Way out of Stanton to Stanway, then along the foot of the slope to reach Wood Stanway from where a steep ascent is made to Stumps Cross. The only real climb on this part of the walk, it is followed by an easy track (the ancient Campden Lane) to Beckbury Camp and to Cromwell's Clump, from where it is said Thomas Cromwell watched as Hailes Abbey was dismantled. Field paths take you to a narrow lane that leads beside orchards to the remains of Hailes Abbey (worth a visit), then across more fields to Winchcombe.

Apart from the steep climb above Wood Stanway, this is an easy, gentle stage. It wanders through a peaceful countryside with soft views to enjoy, not only from the scarp edge, but also from the foot of the hill slope where you gaze off to isolated hills (outliers) such as Alderton Hill near Toddington, and Oxenton Hill north-west of Winchcombe.

* * *

On entering Stanton walk along the village street (note the medieval village cross) and bear left where the road forks, shortly after passing the church. When the road curves to the right strike off to the left on a farm drive, and about 40 yards later you will come to a red, corrugated iron Dutch barn where you bear right over a stile. The continuing footpath skirts the base of the hills, while off to your right spread the lowlands of the Vale of Evesham, broken here and there by groups of individual hills and distant green ridges topped by woodlands. It is a gentle, soft landscape to admire.

This is a fine, easy stretch of the walk, the path leading alongside

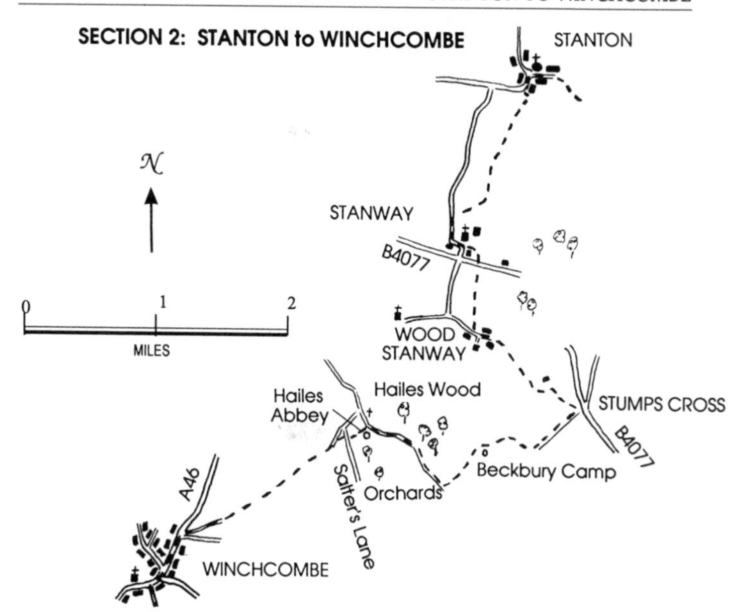

meadows and finally bringing you to the parkland of Stanway House where long avenues of stately chestnut trees throw welcome shade on a hot summer's day. Across the parkland you come to a country lane. Bear left and walk along it into the hamlet of Stanway (1) *(Accommodation)*. Note the huge tithe barn in the ground of Stanway House behind the church, and the thatched cricket pavilion perched on staddle stones on the opposite side of the lane.

The lane winds in front of the parish church and past the fanciful south gatehouse of Stanway House (Grid ref: 061323). A few paces beyond this you leave the lane by a large yew tree and go left towards Stanway Estate Yard. A narrow footpath leads to the left of the Estate Yard, crosses a small meadow and brings you onto another lane, the B4077. Go left for a few paces, then head to the right on a continuation of the Cotswold Way along a path enclosed by a hedge and fence containing a plantation.

This path soon takes you across low-lying fields towards the hamlet of Wood Stanway. (Stanway, which you have just left, is sometimes known as Church Stanway to avoid confusion.) Behind and above the hamlet runs the Cotswold ridge on which you can see a line of individual trees stark against the sky. The route eventually heads up to the left-hand end of these.

On coming to Wood Stanway (a community still, it appears, committed to working the land) head to the left along a narrow road which soon rises past Glebe Farm, then continues as a farm track. Above the farm the path winds up through meadows sloping the hillside, keeping to the left of a line of power cables. Although the path is not always evident on the ground, there are waymarks to guide you on either side of the meadows.

Pass well to the right of a house called Lower Coscombe, then bear left above it and follow the waymarks leading on a diagonal ascent of the hill. There is a narrow line of a path here. This brings you to the head of the slope at the left-hand end of the row of trees seen earlier. Keep to the left of a drystone wall and follow it to the road junction at Stumps Cross (Grid ref: 076303).

Bear right immediately, round the wall, then go through a gate and onto the farm track (Campden Lane, a one-time sheep drove-road), which is to be followed for about half a mile. Before long you will pass a cluster of farm buildings on the right, including a corrugated shed on staddle stones.

Continue along the track until it brings you to a small wood with a gate. Do not go through this gate, but instead turn right onto a path striking north-west alongside the wood by a drystone wall. Pass through a gap in the wall and resume direction, now with a large field on your left. In the bottom corner bear left, still skirting the field boundary. (Big views into the Vale of Evesham again.) Maintaining your direction you will come to the hill fort of Beckbury Camp (2) and the clump of beech trees marking the spot where Thomas Cromwell overlooked the dismantling of Hailes Abbey.

Go through the hunting gate, bear right and descend among the beeches, then below the trees bear left to cross a large meadowland.

With the guidance of waymarks make a gentle diagonal descent to reach an enclosed crossing track. A signpost here gives directions. Turn right and walk downhill along the track among trees, with orchards half seen on the left and Hailes Wood to your right. The track brings you onto a lane. Continue ahead and you will shortly come to Hailes Abbey (3).

A few paces beyond the abbey remains and just before the church, bear left through a kissing gate and into a meadow. Hailes Abbey ruins can be seen over the fence on the left. The meadow footpath brings you to a collection of cottages, then onto a lane where you turn right. This is Salter's Lane, an old saltway and part of a major route from Droitwich to the Thames Valley. (It crosses the Cotswolds here between Hailes and Lechlade.) About 60 yards later go off to the left through a metal field gate and onto a track. As this track begins to rise up the hillside keep alert for a footpath breaking away to the right by a pair of large and elegant oak trees. Follow this path along the edge of a field, then strike off half-left to the far corner where a waymark can be seen.

Go over a stile in the hedge, bear left round the edge of a field for a few yards, then pass through a metal kissing gate into the next meadow. There is no real footpath to be seen on the ground, but you simply head diagonally across a series of undulating meadows in a south-westerly direction (waymarks show the route), with brief views of Winchcombe ahead. You will come to a stile where you bear right onto an enclosed footpath which brings you to a track leading down to the outskirts of Winchcombe. (The enclosed track becomes a narrow metalled road - Puck Pit Lane - bordered by neat trimmed hedges.) On emerging from Puck Pit Lane onto the A46, turn left and walk into Winchcombe, a pleasant small town worth devoting a little time to explore (4) *(Accommodation, & refreshments, shops, post office etc.)*.

Things Seen on the Way:

(1) **Stanway** is even smaller than Stanton; a clutch of buildings in the shadow, so to speak, of the Jacobean manor, Stanway House. It has

Thatched cricket pavilion on staddle stones, Stanway

an air of feudalism about it - the church, the houses, even the trees appear to come under manorial protection. In almost 1,300 years Stanway has changed hands only once (except by inheritance), so perhaps it is not surprising that the community should appear so close knit. The great house is open to the public on set days in summer, but even when closed there are things to be seen: the enormous 14th century tithe barn with its stone-tiled roof; the thatched wooden cricket pavilion set upon staddle stones (given by Sir James Barrie); the bronze St George and the dragon war memorial; the three-storey Jacobean gatehouse with gables adorned with scallop-shell finials; the 12th century church of St Peter (considerably re-stored in 1896), and the flower-bright huddle of vicarage, cottages and farm buildings adding harmony to the scene.

(2) **Beckbury Camp** to the east of Hailes Abbey is the site of an Iron Age hill fort of more than 4 acres. Originally it consisted of a single ditch and rampart, but the ditch has since been filled, although along

the eastern side the rampart can still be made out. Its position on the very scarp edge made it comparatively easy to defend.

3) **Hailes Abbey,** now in the care of the National Trust, was built by Richard, Earl of Cornwall and brother of Henry III, as a thanksgiving for having survived a near shipwreck off the Scillies. The abbey was consecrated in 1251 and monks of the Cistercian Order came to it from Beaulieu. (It was one of the last of all Cistercian abbeys to be built in England.) After Edmund, Earl Richard's second son, had presented the abbey with a phial thought to contain the blood of Christ, Hailes became a place of pilgrimage for nearly 300 years. In 1538 the phial was taken to London where the contents were analysed and announced to be no more than "honey clarified and coloured with saffron." The following year, during the Dissolution of the Monasteries, the abbey was closed, its ornaments taken away, and the buildings sold to a private dealer in 1542. Over the subsequent 200 years various parts of the abbey buildings were used for domestic purposes, yet by the middle fo the 18th century there was practically nothing left. A few graceful archways remain to this day and the foundations in stone can still be seen, while the museum nearby contains sections of beautiful tiled pavement dating from the 16th century. A little farther along the lane, and on the opposite side, Hailes Church, dating from the 12th century (before the abbey was built) is also worth a visit, its medieval wall-paintings are of particular note.

(4) **Winchcombe** is the largest community so far met on the Cotswold Way, but it is still only a small town whose main street is adorned with many typical Cotswold buidings in typical Cotswold stone, although without the overall uniformity and grace exhibited in such places as Campden, Broadway or Stanton. Once an important settlement, Winchcombe was the capital of a Saxon shire and seat of Mercinian royalty. Offa, King of Mercia, dedicated a nunnery here in 790 AD and an abbey was established by his successor, Kenulf, in 811 AD. Kenulf had a son, Kenelm, who was murdered at the behest of his ambitious sister, and as a consequence of Kenelm's death assorted miracles were attributed to him which, in turn, made Winchcombe a place of pilgrimage. The abbey has gone, but the Parish Church of St

Skeleton remains of Hailes Abbey

Peter, built in the 15th century, owes something to abbey money which helped pay for it. Among its more notable features are the 40 gargoyles that adorn the outer walls at gutter level. Elsewhere in the town you will find a pair of wooden stocks outside the Folk Museum, and among its lovely buildings are two or three fine old inns, Tudor houses and cottages with roses growing at their porches. On the continuing route stands Sudeley Castle, Details of which are given under Section 3. *(Tourist Information Office: Town Hall, North Street, Winchcombe. Tel: 602925.)*

* * *

SECTION 3: WINCHCOMBE TO CLEEVE HILL

Distance: $6^1/2$ miles.
Map: O.S. Landranger series; Sheet 163 (Cheltenham & Cirencester Area), 1:50,000.
Accommodation: Cleeve Hill - hotel, youth hostel.
Woodmancote - camping (one and a quarter miles off-route).

On this short, but rather strenuous section of the walk there is a fair amount of height to be gained. It is both a scenic and historically interesting stretch, beginning as you leave Winchcombe with the magnificent Sudeley Castle, whose entrance is on the route, then passing the site of a Roman villa with fine views overlooking Winchcombe's bowl of countryside. There follows a few hundred yards of wandering along a quiet lane before going steeply up through woodland and onto an open hilltop to find the first of the great Neolithic burial chambers on the Cotswold Way, Belas Knap. The route takes you beside the huge mound, then out of its enclosure to pace a wide expanse of country before reaching Cleeve Common. This is a vast moorland-like area of unenclosed land, and on its tour round it the Way makes a long 4 mile loop (not all on this section), whereas a few hundred yards on paths and tracks heading east to west would bring you onto the continuing route! Such is the nature of long-distance walking. However, the gains are substantial, for splendid views are the reward for following the waymarked path. Cleeve Common is above the 1,000 foot contour, and spread just below it on the northern slope is the small village of Cleeve Hill where hotel and youth hostel accommodation can be found.

* * *

Having entered Winchcombe along the A46, follow the road into the centre of town but, shortly before reaching the parish church, turn left into Vineyard Street (signposted to Sudeley Castle). The road crosses the River Isbourne and almost immediately you find the town has

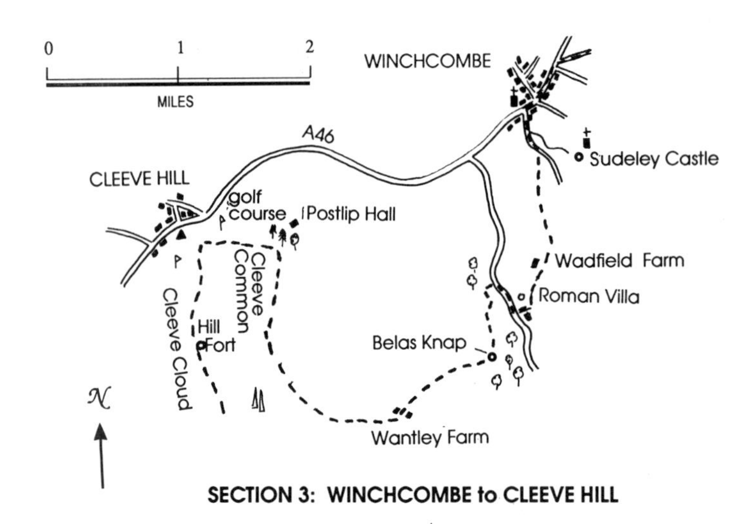

SECTION 3: WINCHCOMBE to CLEEVE HILL

been left behind. Shortly after you pass the entrance to Sudeley Castle (1) the road curves to the right, and as you wander along it, with trees and hedges for company, occasional views show the castle rising above its screen of trees half-left ahead.

Look for a metal field gate on the right with a kissing gate beside it. Go through the gate into a field where waymarks direct you diagonally across to the far side. Midway across the field a telegraph pole bears a footpath sign, and over the brow of the field you cross to a stile in the opposite hedge. Over this stile continue half-right across the next field, on the far side of which you then go over another stile in a hedge to enter a third field. Cross this straight ahead to keep well to the left of a small farm. (Whilst surveying the route waymarking over this stretch was exemplary, with large white discs acting as direction markers.)

Now cross a set of bars, go over a stream and bear right round the edge of the next field. (Away in the valley behind you Sudeley Castle stands proud.) Midway along the hedgerow go through a gap on the right, then bear left and follow the left-hand edge of a rising field. At the top of this maintain direction towards the brow of the hill, which is reached to the left of the handsome early 18th century Wadfield Farm. (This farm enjoys a proud vista of sweeping hill and valley, not a dramatic landscape, but a living, working land, tended and cared for, soft and gently untroubled.)

Pass to the left of the house, hug the right-hand side of the next field and after passing some barns join the track leading to the long, grey row of Humblebee Cottages seen ahead with their woodland backing. Go to the right of the cottages on the continuing track which leads up to a country lane. On the way to it note the clump of conifers enclosed by a wall standing in the field to your right. These conifers mark the site of Wadfield Roman Villa (2) (Grid ref: 024260).

Turn right along the lane for about 400 yards. There are fine views to enjoy as you wander along it, but after the lane begins its descent of the hill, with woods on the left, leave it by way of a stile next to a wooden field gate and take the stone-surfaced path heading uphill through the woods. The way is signposted to Belas Knap and Cleeve Common. A kissing gate takes you out of the woods; you then bear left and follow the field boundary as it rises steadily. On reaching the top of the hilltop field go through another kissing gate and into the enclosure containing Belas Knap Long Barrow (3), a remarkable Neolithic burial chamber and one of the finest sites of the whole walk. An explanation board gives details (Grid ref: 020254).

Having entered the walled enclosure bear right and, after allowing due time to study the barrow, leave it again, now heading a little south of west along the right-hand boundary of a large field and following the line of a drystone wall. At the end of the field walk along a farm track until it dips into a hollow at Wontley Farm. Another track breaks away to the right here. This is the route to follow. It rises through more large open fields and passes beneath a line of high voltage power cables.

Eventually the track takes you through a metal field gate and forks. Take the right branch over a rough moorland-like area brightened with much gorse. This is the start of Cleeve Common (4), the highest

Neolithic burial chamber of Belas Knap

land on the Cotswold Way. (The summit of the Common is 1,083 feet.) Ahead you will notice three tall transmitter towers which will appear and disappear with annoying frequency throughout the long loop of the Common. (**Note** that soon after joining Cleeve Common it is possible to break away south-westwards on a series of tracks and paths south of the towers to rejoin the Way above Prestbury, thus shortcutting the route and missing some of the loveliest views. In emergencies, however, this short cut could be a useful exit from the exposed Common.)

There are many tracks criss-crossing Cleeve Common, but at all junctions there are waymarks to guide you. The direction to maintain is roughly north-west, but on coming to a steep and narrow cleave go down into it and bear right to walk through its bed in a northerly direction. (As is the nature of such cleaves, it can be extremely wet and greasy in inclement weather.)

As the cleave begins to open out with trees below and views growing, you pass to the left of the Washpool, a small pond probably used as a sheep-dip. The path curves round the foot of the hills well to the left of a wall-enclosed woodland. (Postlip Valley lies beyond, with its Elizabethan manor, Postlip Hall, a medieval tithe barn and a Roman Catholic chapel reconsecrated after years of use as a sheep-cot.)

On coming to a stile leading into the Postlip enclosure, do not cross but instead bear left away from it to find a waymark post directing a narrow path steeply up the hillside. As a consolation for the effort of climbing this slope, some fine views are to be had off to the right. Waymarks lead you across the fairways of a golf course, with the village of Cleeve Hill coming into view below. Should you require either refreshment or accommodation, follow signs directing you above the golf club-house. These lead directly into Cleeve Hill. *(Accommodation, refreshments, shop)* (Grid ref: 984268).

Things Seen on the Way:

(1) **Sudeley Castle** dates from the 15th century, but what is seen is a re-building by Ralph Boteler of an earlier 12th century castle. There was an important estate here in Saxon times, and at the time of the Domesday Book it belonged to a great-grandson of Ethelred the Unready. Boteler, who became Lord Chancellor and was made Baron Sudeley, created a magnificent building, but he backed the wrong side in the Wars of the Roses and his property was confiscated by Edward IV. The castle eventually passed into the hands of Henry VIII, but after his death Katherine Parr married Lord Seymour and came to live here. Shortly after giving birth to Mary in 1548 she died and was buried in a lead coffin in St Mary's Chapel. This was desecrated during the Civil War, and the castle badly damaged. Today the remains of the Elizabethan banqueting hall, the tithe barn, Portmore Tower and St Mary's Chapel - all dating from Boteler's time - can be seen, while the restoration of the main castle building is due in considerable part to the generosity of Emma Dent, a local benefactor. The castle and grounds are open to the public and make a fascinating outing.

(2) **Wadfield Roman Villa** above Winchcombe is hidden from walkers on the Cotswold Way by a screen of conifers, and is but one of several Roman buildings that have been found in the district. The site was excavated in 1894-5, having been discovered 30 years previ-

ously by a farm worker whilst ploughing. The villa, occupying an exposed hillside overlooking the north-east, consisted of a courtyard, at least two heated rooms and two others with mosaic pavements. A shed on the site contains sections of floor mosaic.

(3) **Belas Knap** is a fine example of the chambered tombs, or long barrows, of the Severn-Cotswold Group. The name means hilltop beacon, which may identify the mound's use by the Anglo-Saxons, for it stands high on the edge of the wolds above Winchcombe, which was of course occupied during Saxon times. Belas Knap dates from about 3000 BC; a wedge-shaped mound measuring some 178 feet long, 60 feet wide and about 13 feet at its highest point. At its northern end is a false portal with two horns lined with drystone walling and blocked by a massive slab. When it was excavated in 1863 the remains of five children and the skull of an adult were discovered behind the portal. There are two chambers along the eastern side, one on the west and another at the southern end. These are reached by way of shallow passages walled with stones laid in an almost identical fashion to the many drystone walls seen all along the Cotswold Way. No less than 26 burials were found to have been made in the paired north-east and north-west chambers, and the remains of two males and two females in the south-eastern chamber. The 1863 excavation was a rather clumsy affair that also revealed some Roman coins and pottery, and the mound's restoration, apparently, is not altogether accurate. Be that as it may, Belas Knap Long Barrow remains one of the highlights of the Cotswold Way, and will breed hours of speculation as you pace the same wolds that were trod by your Neolithic forebears.

(4) **Cleeve Common** contains the highest point of the Cotswolds. The last expanse of unenclosed land in the region, the Common covers an area of about three square miles and is designated a Grade 1 Site of Special Scientific Interest. Various types of orchid are to be found here, including the bee and frog orchids; glow-worms are frequently seen, and many different types of butterfly are attracted by a diverse assortment of habitats. In spite of the Common's popularity with walkers and golfing enthusiasts, there are large areas that

seem as remote as almost anywhere in Britain. Because of its height, this large upland plateau is often swept by the mists, making it at times a place of cold mystery.

* * *

SECTION 4: CLEEVE HILL TO BIRDLIP

Distance:	15 1/2 miles.
Map:	O.S. Landranger series; Sheet 163 (Cheltenham & Cirencester Area), 1:50,000.
Accommodation:	Birdlip - hotel, b&b.

This is the longest section of the walk, the distance being necessitated by the absence of accommodation actually on the route between Cleeve Hill and Birdlip. It is a splendid stage with some outstanding views. There will be some road walking, but this fortunately is kept to a minimum. Mostly the Way follows the western edge of the Cotswold escarpment high above Cheltenham. Some of it leads through woodland, some through an agricultural landscape and parts are on ragged heath.

It begins by heading south along the scarp edge of Cleeve Common, but when at last this has been deserted you follow a line of woods down to Dowdeswell Reservoir and across the A40 Cheltenham to Oxford road before climbing to woodland again. A choice of route then gives the option of either a woodland and field path walk, or alongside the A436 to Seven Springs, claimed to be one of the sources of the Thames. From here you walk in a long curve round the scarp edge, once more with magnificent views to enjoy, along Charlton Kings Common, past the stubby finger of the Devil's Chimney below Leckhampton Hill and on to Crickley Hill Country Park and its fascinating archaeological site. At last 2 miles of scarp and woodland brings you to Birdlip for overnight accommodation.

* * *

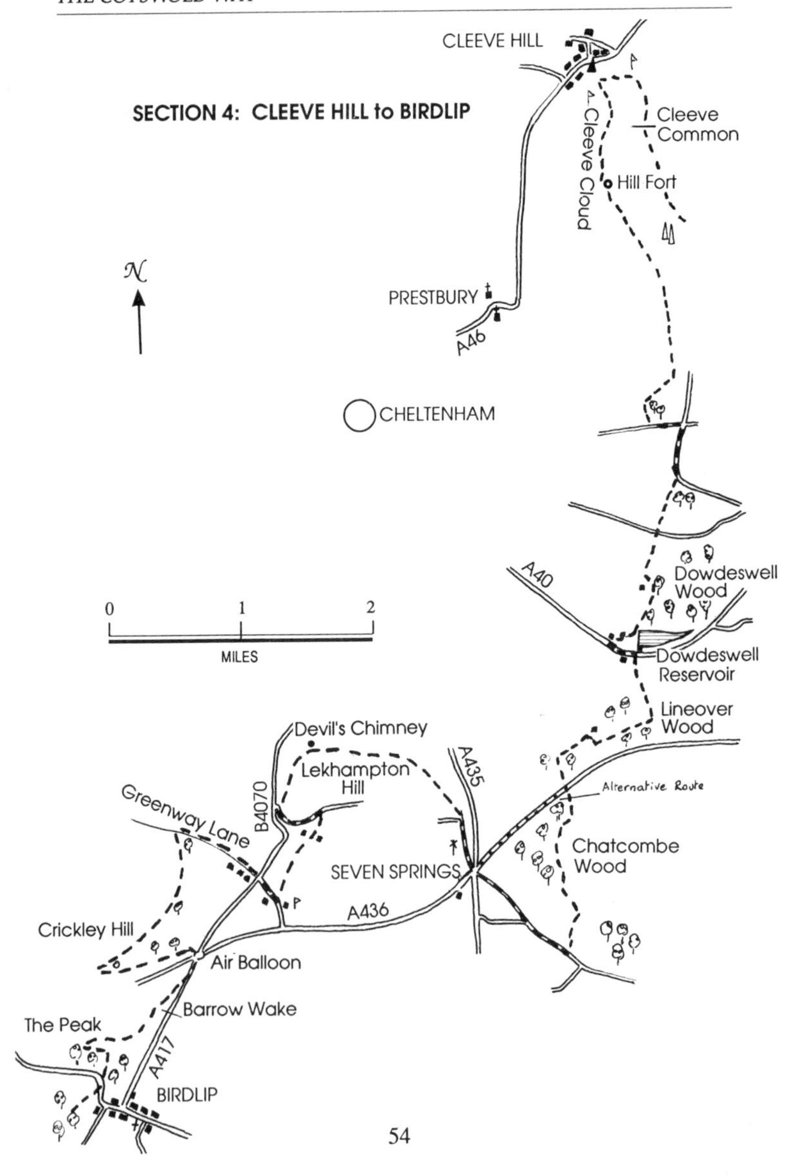
CLEEVE HILL
SECTION 4: CLEEVE HILL to BIRDLIP
Cleeve Common
Cleeve Cloud
Hill Fort
N
PRESTBURY
A46
CHELTENHAM
0
1
2
MILES
A40
Dowdeswell Wood
Dowdeswell Reservoir
Lineover Wood
Devil's Chimney
Lekhampton Hill
A435
B4070
Greenway Lane
Alternative Route
Chatcombe Wood
SEVEN SPRINGS
A436
Crickley Hill
Air Balloon
Barrow Wake
The Peak
A417
BIRDLIP

From Cleeve Hill village return to the golf course on Cleeve Common and follow Cotswold Way signs (right) on a traverse of the north-western hillside (views down to the sprawl of Bishop's Cleeve below), before waymarks direct you up to the trig point on the summit of Cleeve Hill. (There is also a topograph showing points of interest in the long views.) Bear right away from the trig point following the series of waymarked posts across the golf course, now heading due south along the western side of the Common. (It is almost impossible to give precise directions because of the number of paths and golf course trails. Cotswold Way waymarks are maintained in good order and are your best guide.)

The Way now leads along the rocky western edge of the escarpment on Cleeve Cloud above woods, and with the steep crags of Castle Rock making a fine show. Views are over Cheltenham, and as you approach an Iron Age hill fort, so you can see the farm buildings of Nutterswood below. After passing the rough undulations of the hill fort earthworks a track comes up from the valley to your right, but you continue ahead and follow a fence and a wall until it brings you to a large Cleeve Common notice-board. Beside the notice there is a metal field gate. Go through this and follow a track among hawthorns. (Note the transmitter masts once more half-left ahead.)

When you leave the hawthorns the route bears right a little to join another path heading to the left among yet more hawthorn bushes and dropping downhill steeply in places. Go through a gateway then, ignoring a footpath off to the right, continue ahead to find a narrow path which you join to climb leftwards. It leads beside a fence, soon curves right and passes through a wooden gate onto a track following along the lower edge of a beechwood. Cheltenham is clearly seen off to the right at the foot of the slope.

This track makes a lengthy traverse of the hillside, sometimes rising a little, but mostly keeping on a gentle course along an even contour. Coming out of a section enclosed by bushes, go through a wooden gate and bear right through gorse, then find a crossing path which you join heading to the left. This contours over a rough patch of hillside. Over a stile bear left for a few yards uphill to a crossing track where you go to the right and head downhill.

The track brings you to a metal field gate at the top of a narrow, surfaced lane. Go through the gate and branch off left on a footpath aiming alongside some woods with a large meadowland stretching away to your right. At this point fine views show across the valley to the continuing Cotswold ridge.

On coming to the end of the woods bear left along a narrow country lane guarded by a line of superb beech trees. At a minor crossroads turn right. This lane also has a row of ancient pollarded beech trees alongside it. When it curves sharply leftwards leave the lane and continue straight ahead, over a stile, then walk forward against the right-hand boundary of a level meadowland, following a drystone wall with woods seen ahead. When the meadow ends maintain direction. Although the wall has finished, a fence continues. You will come to a stile, cross a very narrow lane and continue down the next field towards some barns. When the right-hand hedge swings more to the right, a waymark directs the route half-left across the field towards a stile about 30 yards to the left of the barns. High voltage power cables cross overhead.

Cross the stile and a farm drive beneath the power cables, climb over a second stile opposite to find a path which now heads among trees down towards a valley. This narrow footpath leads alongside the Dowdeswell Estate Plantation. It is very steep in places (greasy in wet weather, when you will need to exercise caution), but with a number of steps having been cut into the slope to ease the gradient.

Near the foot of the slope Dowdeswell Reservoir can be seen to the left (Grid ref: 987197). On coming out of the trees cross a sluice and follow a drive as it curves to the right and brings you to the busy A40 road. Bear left and walk alongside the road to pass the Reservoir Inn *(Refreshments)*. When the road curves leftwards near the tall grey reservoir building, break away to the right on a track signposted to Seven Springs and Leckhampton Hill.

A series of easily identified waymarks lead up green sloping meadows, then over a stile onto an enclosed path beside Lineover Wood. At first surfaced with stones, it then becomes a more narrow and steeply climbing path, crosses a stile and heads along the boundary of another meadow to a higher section of Lineover Wood draped on the north-west escarpment. The Way now takes you over two more stiles and into the wood, which is successor to a forest mentioned in documents as being here in the 9th century.

The delightful woodland path makes a steady descending traverse of the slope amid a riot of birdsong, and you finally emerge near Old Dole Farm (with a small reservoir below it). Go up the sloping meadow, beneath power cables, to the top left-hand corner where a gate will be found among a group of trees. Through the gate bear half-right to skirt the lower edge of a steep hillside meadow, but soon break away left onto a narrow path climbing diagonally up to the wood-crowned crest. On reaching this join a short track heading through the strip of Wistley Plantation, cross a large exposed hilltop field and come to the A436.

There now follows a choice of route to Seven Springs (1). The first is straightforward, but decidedly unpleasant in heavy traffic. It is to turn right and walk along the road for almost exactly a mile to reach the staggered Seven Springs crossroads. There is no footpath and traffic is often heavy along this stretch. The alternative route adds about a mile to the overall distance, and is described below.

Alternative (waymarked) route: Cross the A436 with care and walk ahead on a drive beside Chatcombe Wood. When the drive curves right continue ahead on a track which soon enters the left-hand edge of the wood. This track can be very muddy at times. Beyond the wood continue along the left headland of a large field. Just before coming to a pylon go through a gate on the left, and head diagonally across the next field, passing beneath the power lines and alongside a pond. On the far side of the field turn right on a track among trees. Two fields later join a narrow road and bear right. In 1/2 mile the road makes a sharp left turn. Now go on ahead on a track which leads to the Seven Springs crossroads. (**Note** that the Seven Springs Inn is found a few paces along the continuation of the A436, should you be in need of liquid refreshment at this point.If you arrived at the crossroads along the A435, cross the road with caution to the continuing Cotswold Way sign opposite. It directs you to the right along a narrow road. If, however, you reached the crossroads via the alternative, Chatcombe Wood route, cross over - also with great care - and take the narrow side road almost opposite. You will soon pass a windpump in the field on the left.

When the road curves left, continue straight ahead on an enclosed footpath signposted to Leckhampton Hill. At a junction of paths bear left and follow the left-hand boundary of an enclosed rectangular field. This path then enters a spinney and out again along the scarp edge. (Off to your right the transmitter towers on Cleeve Common may still be seen, together with Cheltenham below.)

This is a fine stretch with splendid views overlooking the Severn Vale; the path rising along the scarp edge of Charlton Kings Common to Hartley Hill and, among gorse bushes with numerous hollows where ragstone has been extracted for drystone walling, onto the flat-topped Leckhampton Hill with its trig point and more fine views. Continue along the scarp edge, but look for a sign on the right offering a short diversion to see the Devil's Chimney, a noted pinnacle of rock projecting from the lower shelf of the scarp face (2) (Grid ref: 946184). (This sign was found to be broken on my last visit.)

The Cotswold Way continues its scarp edge path and descends to a narrow country lane where you turn left. Near the crown of the hill bear right on a bridleway to Ullenwood and Shurdington Hill. The bridleway goes along the right-hand boundary of a field beside elder, hawthorn and pine, through a gateway and onto a track with a plantation on the left. Continue down the track.

The track leads to a minor road. Turn right and walk to a crossroads, passing Ullenwood Manor on your left (now a training centre for the disabled). Cross the B4070 and go ahead along Greenway Lane, another of the Cotswold sheep drove roads running straight as a die between neat hedges and drystone walls. If you gaze over your right shoulder you will see the steep cut of the scarp edge and the Devil's Chimney standing clear almost a mile away (although it's taken 2 miles to walk from it). Along Greenway Lane you pass a former army camp, and soon after come to a beech grove with

Shurdington Long Barrow in the field before it. When the lane bears slightly left, leave it to go up some steps on the left onto a continuing path along the edge of the beechwood. Once again the Way leads along the scarp edge with yet more lovely views to the west.

The path leads through a narrow strip of beechwoods that help frame the views and diffuse the light into slanting pillars; then you come to Crickley Hill Country Park with its hill fort - complete with observation platform built to ease problems of erosion where excavations have taken place (3). From the observation platform continue ahead to the end of a promontory (beautiful views), then return alongside a drystone wall, cutting back, then sloping out of the hill fort area. Keep beside the wall, beyond which you go ahead into beechwoods, eventually coming out near the busy roundabout at the Air Balloon pub (Grid ref: 935161) *(Refreshments).*

Cross over with care and pass to the left of the pub to follow the Gloucester road. Having passed a telephone kiosk and a bus shelter the pavement dips and a waymarked, narrow path heads away to the right among trees to bring you onto the scarp edge once more. The path leads you on a delightful switchback course along Barrow Wake, enjoying broad panoramas which include the Vale of Gloucester, May Hill, the Black Mountains and Brecon Beacons beyond, and the curving line of the wolds ahead. (It was here, along Barrow Wake, that a century ago a quarryman exposed a female burial containing a silver brooch, bronze owls, a decorated bucket and a richly ornamated bronze mirror. These finds are to be seen in the Gloucester City Museum.) You will come to a topograph giving details of the region's geological formations, and another of the usual panoramic variety.

A barbed wire fence leads the path into a field, and this in turn takes you into a mixed woodland. Bear right. On coming to a junction of paths continue ahead for a further 70 yards to a promontory descriptively known as The Peak, where lovely secluded views are to be had. (Originally the Cotswold Way climbed the steep path below The Peak, but was re-routed from Crickley Hill.) Backtrack from The Peak to the path junction and take the right-hand branch winding among the trees, bringing you to a woodland track. This leads directly to the road immediately below the village of Birdlip (4) *(Accomodation, refreshments, shop)* (Grid ref: 925145). To reach the village walk uphill for about 400 yards. To continue the walk, cross the road to where the path descends among trees.

Things Seen on the Way:

(1) **Seven Springs,** just off the route of the Cotswold Way, is often claimed to be the earliest source of the Thames (a moot point, since it is the River Churn which begins here, and that is only a tributary of the Thames). The springs leak from the water-table beneath Hartley Hill and are to be found a short distance down the A436 below the roundabout in a tree-clad hollow to the north of the road.

(2) **The Devil's Chimney** is one of the major landmarks of the walk; a craggy finger of rock projecting from the second terrace of the scarp face below Leckhampton Hill above Cheltenham. Throughout the 18th century extensive quarrying took place on Leckhampton Hill, and the exposed pinnacle is a result of this industry. Apparently local quarrymen trimmed the Chimney as part of a hoax, while one of Cheltenham's legends has it that Old Nick was buried by falling rocks when he was working his mischief, and the Chimney marks the spot where he lies. In more recent times repair work was necessary to arrest the effects of erosion which threatened the landmark with collapse. Climbing the pinnacle is now prohibited, but for years it made a popular scramble - the record stands at 13 people on the top at one time!

(3) **Crickley Hill** is the site of one of the Cotswolds' great archaeological discoveries. Excavations began in 1969. It has been found that in Neolithic times more than 3 acres of the hill were occupied as a camp, consisting of a single ditch and a bank, during the period 4,000-3,000 BC. A second occupation took place about 700 BC by Iron Age settlers when 9 acres of the hill were used for housing, the storage of crops and livestock pens. A rampart and palisaded walk-way surrounded the camp, and a six foot ditch was dug. A third camp was made here following a period when Crickley Hill had been abandoned by these first Iron Age settlers, and during this final

occupation round houses were built. This term of settlement ended with destruction by fire. On the observation platform a series of explanation panels describe the various stages of occupation.

(4) **Birdlip** stands on the edge of the escarpment on the course of the Roman Ermin Street (or Ermin Way), which ran from Gloucester (Glevum) to Cirencester (Corinium). A convenient overnight stop on the long walk.

* * *

SECTION 5: BIRDLIP TO PAINSWICK

Distance:	7 miles.
Maps:	O.S. Landranger series; Sheets 163 (Cheltenham & Cirencester Area) and 162 (Gloucester & Forest of Dean Area), 1:50,000.
Accommodation:	Cooper's Hill - b&b, camping. Cranham Corner - b&b, camping. Painswick - hotel, b&b, camping.

This is another lovely walk, much of it through woodland but with panoramic viewpoints to enjoy too, such as that from the head of the cheese-rolling slope at Cooper's Hill, and also from the hill fort on Painswick Beacon. Painswick itself is another of the gems of the Cotswolds, an old market town built of the whitest of all local stones, famed for its clipped churchyard yews and table tombs, but with much more to admire in its maze of back streets.

The Way leaves Birdlip Hill and takes to woods immediately, cutting round the northern scarp slope with intimate vistas through the trees, then up steeply onto Cooper's Hill. More woodlands continue the walk on a south-westerly course to pass above Prinknash Abbey, then you cross the A46 at Cranham Corner and head out to the common land and manicured fairways of a golf course below Painswick Beacon, before catching sight of Paradise on the final mile downhill to Painswick.

Refreshments are available below Cooper's Hill.

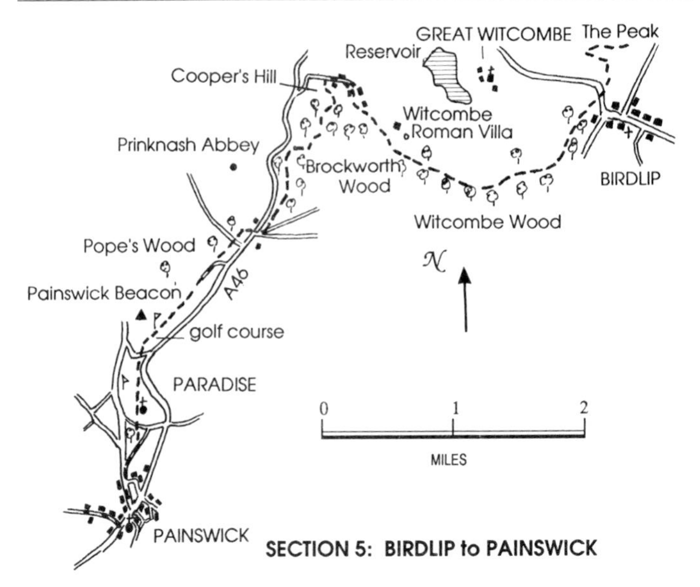

SECTION 5: BIRDLIP to PAINSWICK

The continuing path heads south from the road which descends Birdlip Hill and is found directly opposite the woodland track leading from The Peak. The path slopes down among trees and undergrowth with views into the valley where Brockworth lies in a sprawl beyond Witcombe Reservoir. On coming to a crossing path head to the left, with acres of fields and meadows on the right sweeping towards that reservoir. The path forks and you bear left, rising easily through Witcombe Wood. At a broad cross-track bear right, and at the next crossing go straight ahead.

There are many paths and tracks in the beechwoods as you curve round the 'combe' of Witcombe, but confusion is avoided by generous, yet not overly intrusive, waymarking. On occasion the correct route deserts a broad track for a minor path, so remain alert for signs. If the onward route is not obvious at any stage, simply look for a guiding CW arrow. (Ignore any arrows that do not bear the white spot denoting the Cotswold Way.)

At one stage the Way leads alongside a gamekeeper's fence, with pheasants seen in abundance on both sides. At another point you will pass the stone pillars of an estate gateway. Some of the route follows a bridleway and, as is common along such tracks, this is often rather muddy and churned by horses' hooves. Fallow deer roam these woodlands and lone walkers stepping lightly may be rewarded by a sighting. Often, as the route leads along the woodland edge, fine views are given across the reservoir to a curve of folding hills and meadows, and in the coombe to the right, near Cooper's Hill Farm, is the site of a Roman villa (1).

On the outer edge of the woods a track brings you to a solitary cottage with a splendid view. Shortly after this you go through a gateway and onto a narrow metalled drive to pass a number of cottages, one of which advertises teas and snacks (The Haven Tea Garden) *(Refreshments)*. Ignore the footpath sign pointing sharply to the left and continue along the lane. Opposite Primrose Cottage, at the entrance to a house called Stoneleigh, bear left to find a track which leads to a footpath rising into more woods. Go through a kissing gate and continue to climb to a junction of paths where you bear left and rise among some lovely beech trees onto the open sunny glade of Cooper's Hill (2) on which there stands a maypole (Grid ref: 892146). Glorious views are to be had over Brockworth and Gloucester, the distant curve of the Cotswold escarpment and, far off, the Malvern Hills. It is claimed that the Black Mountains can also be seen from here.

The route continues now through more woodland. With your back to the view as you stand beside the maypole, you will see two paths ahead. Take that which is half-right and follow it into the woods. On coming to a junction of tracks take the lower of two going off to the left. Brockworth and Buckholt Woods are linked by a short and narrow 'corridor' which is clearly waymarked. Designation as a National Nature Reserve acts as a protection for much of these woodlands, and in springtime they display a rich profusion of shade-loving plants amidst the birch, sycamore, beech and ash.

Almost as soon as you enter the second wood the path forks. Take the left branch and continue. At the next fork take the right-hand option ahead.The Way broadens and more alternative paths and tracks are seen, but at each junction there are waymarks to direct you. Eventually the path brings you downhill among more fine beech trees, with a glimpse now and then of views between them off to the right, and you come to an unclassified road. Turn right and in a few paces you reach a junction with the A46 (Grid ref: 883131). This is sometimes referred to as Cranham Corner, sometimes as Prinknash Corner *(Accommodation)*. Prinknash Abbey lies down the slope to the north (3).

Cross the A46 road half-left ahead to find a continuing footpath with Cotswold Way (CW) waymarks directing you once more into woodland. For about 100 yards you wander beside a drystone wall, then leave it to bear left up a slope along a minor path. Within a few paces cross another road (an unclassified road that leads to Gloucester) and walk straight on along the track which runs parallel to the A46 heading south-west.

This woodland (Pope's Wood) is part of Buckholt Wood Nature Reserve and has a fine selection of deciduous trees and ground-covering plants. The track leads through it to a narrow metalled lane which in turn brings you out of the woods, at last, and onto a golf course. Waymarks lead across the golf course, usually on a visible path or track and maintaining direction to the left of the attractive undulations of Painswick Beacon, alternatively known as Painswick Hill (Grid ref: 868121) (4). It is worth making a slight diversion onto the summit of the hill (931 feet) for the views.

Keeping to the waymarked route, views are given off to the left (south and east) across a green valley with yet more woods on the far side. On coming to a narrow lane cutting across the golf course bear left along it and, a few paces later, go to the right on a broad track signposted to Painswick. Leave the track for a footpath half-left ahead and pass Catsbrain Quarry. The Way leads along the edge of the hill slope, once more in woods but with more lovely tree-framed views to enjoy.

When you emerge from the woods cross an open stretch of golf

The Devil's Chimney - symbol of The Cotswold Way (Section 4)

course fairway to the right-hand corner of a churchyard wall opposite. Now continue with the wall to your left, pass a fine-looking church and beyond the wall above the hamlet of Paradise (so-called, it is said, because Charles I, during the Civil War, thought the little hamlet to be just like the paradise of his dreams), to cross a further open space half-left to a woodland corner. Here a narrow lane takes you to a junction with the B4073 where you turn left and stroll downhill into Painswick.

Follow Gloucester Street towards the centre of town. On coming to a crossroads turn right into New Street. For a more interesting detour through the town cross over New Street into Bisley Street, then head to the right into Friday Street, along St Mary's Street and on to the gracefully spired St Mary's church. Rejoin the main route in New Street on the other side of the church by wandering through the churchyard and out at the lych gate (5) *(Accommodation, refreshments, shops, post office etc.)* (Grid ref: 866097).

Things Seen on the Way:

(1) **Witcombe Roman Villa** stands on the spring-line near the foot of the northern slopes between Birdlip Hill and Cooper's Hill. Dating from the 1st century it was built on land exploited by Iron Age man, and excavations have unearthed sections of a bath house with fine mosaics pictorially depicting seascapes as well as fish. The site is occasionally open to the public.

(2) **Cooper's Hill** is noted not just for its superb viewpoint, but also for the Whitsuntide festival of cheese-rolling down its excessively steep grass slope. (The festivities are now held on Spring Bank Holiday Monday each year.) Contestants plunge heroically from the maypole down the slope in pursuit of a mock cheese, the winner taking home a real 7lb Double Gloucester as the prize. In about 500 BC Cooper's Hill was part of a large Iron Age encampment.

(3) **Prinknash Abbey,** built as recently as 1972, looks more like a modern office block than a Benedictine monastery. Starkly rectangular and flat-roofed, it is in brazen contrast to the small gabled mansion that had housed the community since 1928. Whilst the foundations

Cotswold view from Paradise, near Painswick (Section 5)

of the new abbey were being dug, rich clay beds were discovered. This clay now forms the basis of the well known Prinknash pottery that is the abbey's major financial support. The abbey lies half a mile off the route. *(Refreshments).*

(4) **Painswick Beacon** has many other names - Painswick Hill, The Castles, Castle Godwyn and Kimsbury Hill. Overlooking Gloucester and the Severn Vale it was settled as a hill fort by late Iron Age tribes, used in 1052 as a temporary camp by Earl Godwyn (a Saxon leader in conflict with the Earl of Mercia), and again in 1643 by Royalist forces following the lifting of the Siege of Gloucester. The 250 acres of common land are speckled with birches and manicured as a golf course.

(5) **Painswick** is another old market town and, like Chipping Campden at the start of the walk, a small one at that. But unlike the honey-gold of Campden, Painswick's stone is strangely white, or light grey in colour. As a result the houses appear a little more formal than those of Campden, yet Painswick has much of merit and is worthy of more than a transitory glance. New Street is one of the oldest, in fact it dates from the 13th century, but other streets - notably those to the north-east of the church - are worth walking to see. Friday Street indicates the siting of the Friday market, while Bisley Street, the original main street when Painswick was merely a village named Wicke, has a collection of splendid old buildings, among the oldest in the town. In common with several other towns visited on the Cotswold Way, Painswick owes its elegance to the cloth trade, at the height of which 25 mills were being powered by local streams flowing through the valley. The Parish Church of St Mary has a lofty spire 174 feet high, which calls from afar. The rebuilding of the church dates from the 14th century, the tower from 1430, the spire from 1632. In the Civil War Royalists attacked the town and the church was damaged by both fire and cannonballs, marks of which are evident to this day. The churchyard is noted for its wonderful clipped yews, its Renaissance-style table tombs and the more recent lych gate whose timbers, decorated with carvings of bells and music, came from the belfry roof after the spire fell in and damaged it in 1883. Each

Clipped yews and table tombs - Painswick

September the Clipping Ceremony takes place round the church - not the clipping of the churchyard yews, but a ceremony based on the Saxon word for embracing *(ycleping)* when the congregation joins hands to encircle the church whilst singing a special hymn.

* * *

SECTION 6: PAINSWICK TO MIDDLE YARD (KING'S STANLEY)

Distance: 9½miles.
Map: O.S. Landranger series; Sheet 162 (Gloucester & Forest of Dean Area), 1:50,000.
Accommodation: Randwick - b&b (half a mile off-route).
King's Stanley - camping.
Middle Yard - b&b.

Open meadows, woodland shade, a sloping birch-bright common (Edge Common) and some of the finest views of the whole Cotswold Way ensure that this stage is both memorable and full of variety.

Leaving Painswick the route heads westward over undulating farmland, across the Gloucester to Stroud road and up to Scottsquar Hill with its quarry remains and a glorious view back to Painswick. It then passes along the edge of an extensive stretch of woodland broken here and there with occasional views north and west, before climbing onto the jutting prow of Haresfield Beacon where a vast panorama, lit by the meanderings of the River Severn, lies stretched before you. This is a green belvedere to sit and enjoy; a fine picnic spot.

From Haresfield Beacon the Way now breaks to the south, making a short diversion onto a neighbouring hilltop spur in order to exploit more of the magnificent vista before dropping among ancient woodlands again well to the west of Stroud. Stroud dominates a bowl of countryside above the River Frome, but the route keeps its distance and remains distinctly rural, passing through one or two outlying villages, crossing the Frome and the Stroudwater Canal and, at King's Stanley, ending in a final meadowland stroll to Middle Yard below wooded Pen Hill.

This is a lovely walk, the waymarks are mostly reliable and the paths clear. Take your time over it and make this a full day's journey, then you will be able to enjoy the views, the plants and the birds around you to full advantage.

* * *

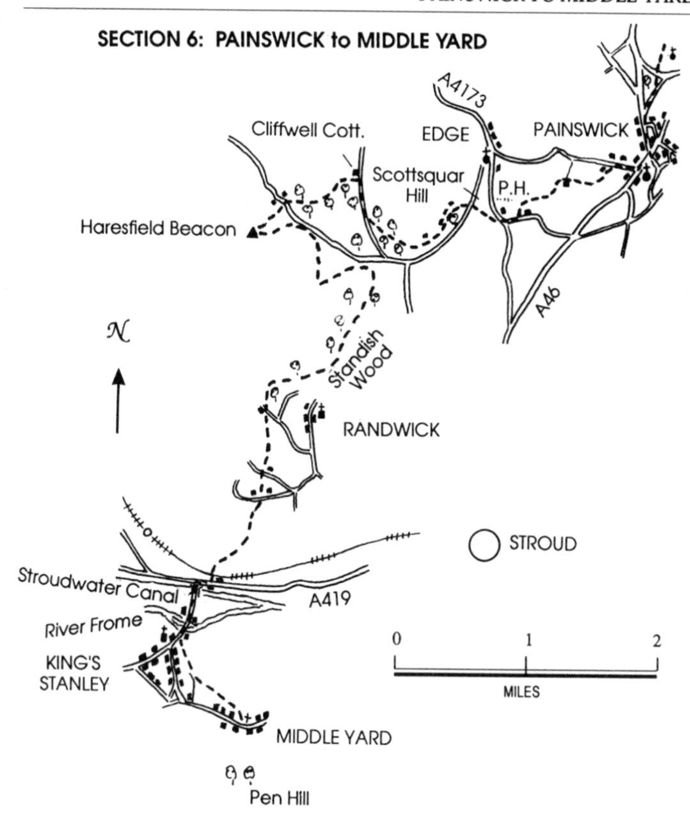

Opposite the lych gate on the New Street side of St Mary's church in Painswick, a narrow lane breaks away to the north-west. This is Edge Road. Wander uphill along it, enjoying pleasant views off to the left as you gain height. After about 300 yards strike off to the left over a stile and into Hambutts Field (owned by the Open Spaces Society). Wander down the left-hand edge, go over a stile and along an enclosed footpath at the back of some houses, emerging to an open sloping meadow. Go down the centre of this, but half-way down branch off half-left to a stile near the corner of a tennis court. Continue along the left-hand edge of a field. After about 50 yards veer half-right to the bottom right-hand corner, and cross another stile. The continuing path takes you over a stream and onto a track by the 17th century grey stone Washbrook Farm, a former cloth mill that later changed to milling flour but does neither now. (Grid ref: 857096).

Pass to the right of Washbrook Farm, then go left on a track towards the farm outbuildings. Continue along the right-hand side of two large barns. Beyond the second of these a grassy track leads up a slope, but after a few paces go over a stile on your left and follow a narrow path into some rather overgrown and tangled woods. Cross a footbridge over a stream, then up some wood-braced steps into a meadow. Bear left through this to find a stile in the wire fence ahead. Pause here for a moment to look back and enjoy a lovely view of Painswick with its backdrop of wooded hills.

Over a stile bear left and find a few steps leading through a gap in a wall by some trees. (Jenkins Farm stands nearby off to the left.) You will come onto a narrow lane where you go uphill to the right, shortly to join the Gloucester-Stroud road near the Edgemoor Inn *(Refreshments).* Cross the road straight ahead and climb a narrow footpath, at first bullied by marauding hedges. After about 100 yards the path forks. Take the right branch and then right again at a crossing path. (This is Edge Common where a number of CW waymarks are found on special posts.) Wander along the hillside among scatterings of silver birch (a bird-happy stretch), then break away leftwards on a narrow path winding gently to ascend Scottsquar Hill, on the top of which you can enjoy a truly delightful view towards Painswick gleaming white in the sun, and the backing hills rolling green and pleasant to create a landscape of some splendour (Grid ref: 846093). Several varieties of orchid and herbs grow on Edge Common, and the hillside attracts a summer population of various butterflies.

Scottsquar Hill has been quarried in the past, and between the hilltop and a narrow country lane to the west, the continuing path rises and falls and winds among rough undulations. Cross the lane and go straight ahead where the footpath is signposted to Haresfield Beacon, 3 kilometres.

From Edge Common, Painswick is seen nestling in its bowl of meadows and trees

A narrow path descends through woods and brings you to a farm track where you bear left. After passing two or three houses the track narrows, and then continues once more through the National Trust owned Stockend Wood. The track is a bridleway and can be extremely muddy in places. Below the wood, and unseen from the Way, is yet another site of a Roman villa. Eventually the bridleway emerges onto a narrow lane where you bear right to be gifted, almost immediately, with more fine views to the right across an indented coombe to the curving escarpment. Scattered below among green, soft meadows are typical Cotswold stone cottages and farms, toy-like in the distance.

A short distance along the lane you come to Cliffwell Cottage, named after the well beside which it is set. (The inscription on the well-head is worth quoting:

'Whoer the Bucketful upwindeth, let him bless God, who water findest. Yet water here but small availeth. Go seek that well which never failest.')

A track leads up to the left of the cottage hedge. Follow this - a fine track curving round the scarp edge among woods, but often gaining lovely views. On a bend in the track you pass a stone commemorating the raising of the Siege of Gloucester on September 5th, 1643 by the troops of Charles I. But why this commemorative stone should be called Cromwell's Stone is unclear.

On coming to a small road opposite Ring Hill Farm bear left for a few paces, then go to the right, through a metal field gate and along a track winding uphill beside a Dutch barn. At another field gate take the path along the right-hand side of a fence, over a stile and on to the trig point at the promontory end of Ring Hill, known here as Haresfield Beacon (1) (Grid ref: 820089). This exquisite spot, one end of a 10 acre hill fort, rewards with a magnificent broad panorama overlooking the Vale of Gloucester, the River Severn, and the Forest of Dean rimming the horizon. The Severn glistens and gleams as it sweeps in huge ox-bows. There are green vales and green meadows below, woods and hedgerows darkening the landscape with strips and cloud-like shadows far off. There are distant towns and villages and isolated farms, but each in its place. It is all so orderly and set out in artistic proportions - a lovely, gentle, very English landscape.

Return from the trig point, this time along the southern edge with the slope falling to your right, and note across the indented vale another projecting spur which you will visit next.

The path takes you among trees and then out to the edge of a road, but without going onto it cut away to the right on a waymarked descent of a series of wood-braced steps and a path which winds left along the lower terrace of hillside. The path soon begins to reclaim lost height and brings you to a large open meadowland. Bear half-right across this to reach a topograph with more superb views to enjoy, complementing those of Haresfield Beacon a short distance to the north-west.

Return from the topograph on a faint path going half-right ahead (north-east), as you stand with your back to the view. The path takes you to the National Trust car park at Cripplegate, which you leave by a gap in the wall. A track then leads into Standish Wood, an ancient wood mentioned in a document of 1297. Almost at once the track forks three ways. Take the left-hand trail and follow this deeply into the woods. There are many alternative side tracks and junctions but, on coming to each one, Cotswold Way (CW) waymarks direct you along the correct path. Later you join a bridleway which heads downhill and emerges from the woods. As you leave the trees, Stroud is seen sprawling in its valley.

Coming to the head of a small road which leads to Randwick, cross directly ahead, go through a gate into a meadow and follow a stone wall beyond which there are more fine views. Pass through a second gate and continue until the short left-hand wall finishes, then bear half-left to locate a stone stile at the top end of another wall and take the footpath through Three Bears Wood.

At the end of this small woodland veer left on a narrow lane by some houses (Westrip). Soon you go right over another stone stile into a meadowland with the path going straight ahead. The path, stile and waymarks lead down to more houses on yet another narrow road. Here turn right and walk uphill for about 200 yards, then bear left over a stile and cut through a field to a squeeze stile found beneath an oak tree. Continue in the same direction, go beneath some power cables and, in a dip, cross a stile by a field gate then follow the left-hand boundary hedge of the field beyond.

After two sides of the field you come to another squeeze stile. Maintain direction through two more fields, then find a footbridge leading from the middle of the left-hand boundary hedge of the third field, over the Stroud-Gloucester railway line and down the edge of a school sports field. On coming to the A419 opposite a garden centre, turn right and walk along the pavement to a road junction with a dimple roundabout. Cross with care and go down the road sign-posted to King's Stanley and Ryeford. This takes you over the Stroudwater Canal (2) and, soon after, the meagre River Frome which is guarded by King's Stanley Mill (3) on the edge of King's Stanley village (Grid ref: 813043).

On the left of the road now, waymarks take you over a stile and along the left-hand edge of a long field. Wander along this - parallel with a line of houses below. At the end cross a stile and maintain direction through a second field, then over another stile the path divides. Take the top, left-hand option along the upper edge of a sloping meadow. The way leads along the boundary of a farm and comes to a farm road near some barns. Cross to a stile leading into a field which you cross diagonally. Waymarks and stiles lead over three more fields, then out onto a road at Middle Yard, next to King's Stanley Baptist Church (Grid ref: 820032) *(Accommodation; refreshments half a mile NW).*

Things Seen on the Way:

(1) **Haresfield Beacon** is a promontory viewpoint at the tip of Ring Hill, on which a hill fort once stood. The Romans were here, and at the eastern end of Ring Hill excavations unearthed traces of a Roman building and a pot containing nearly 3,000 coins.

(2) **Stroudwater Canal** was opened in 1779 to service the industrialised Stroud Valley. It is only 8 miles long, but it links Stroud town with the navigable River Severn at Upper Framilode by way of a dozen locks.

(3) **King's Stanley Mill** stands on the south bank of the River Frome. A five-storey brick and stone building, it was constructed in 1811 and its great looms were originally powered by no less than five water-wheels. (These gave way to steam power in 1827.) Within its first 20 years the mill employed almost 1,000 workers.

* * *

SECTION 7: MIDDLE YARD TO DURSLEY

Distance:	$6^1/2$ miles.
Map:	O.S. Landranger series; Sheet 162 (Gloucester & Forest of Dean Area), 1:50,000.
Accommodation:	Nympsfield - b&b, camping (half a mile off-route). Dursley - hotel.

This short stage tends to be rather strenuous at times, with a fair amount of height to be gained and lost. There are interesting archaeological sites to be seen, more extensive views, woodland walks and that finest of all outliers - Cam Long Down - to be crossed.

Climbing out of Middle Yard, the Way soon plunges into glorious beechwoods for a long traverse of hillside, but when it finally emerges onto Frocester Hill near the Nympsfield long barrow, a splendid open panorama comes as a welcome gift. Cam Long Down and Cam Peak (or Peaked Down according to the Ordnance Survey) are seen clearly from here: two isolated hills (outliers) that have become separated from the main escarpment, they appear like landlocked islands rising from the Vale of Berkeley to the south-west. The route passes near Hetty Pegler's Tump, another Neolithic long barrow, and Uleybury promontory fort which was created during the Iron Age. Short diversions are recommended to look at both these ancient sites.

The waymarked route slopes down the steep scarp face, then cuts west-ward to make the ascent of Cam Long Down, and over this to Peaked Down before dropping into Dursley, a busy little town wedged between the wolds.

* * *

Where the path brings the Cotswold Way into Middle Yard beside King's Stanley Baptist Church, turn left and walk along the road for about 30 yards, then cross to the right and go up a narrow lane. It curves a little to the left, and here you branch off to the right on a continuing drive, passing a house and coming to an enclosed foot-path rising steadily towards some woods. The path brings you to a

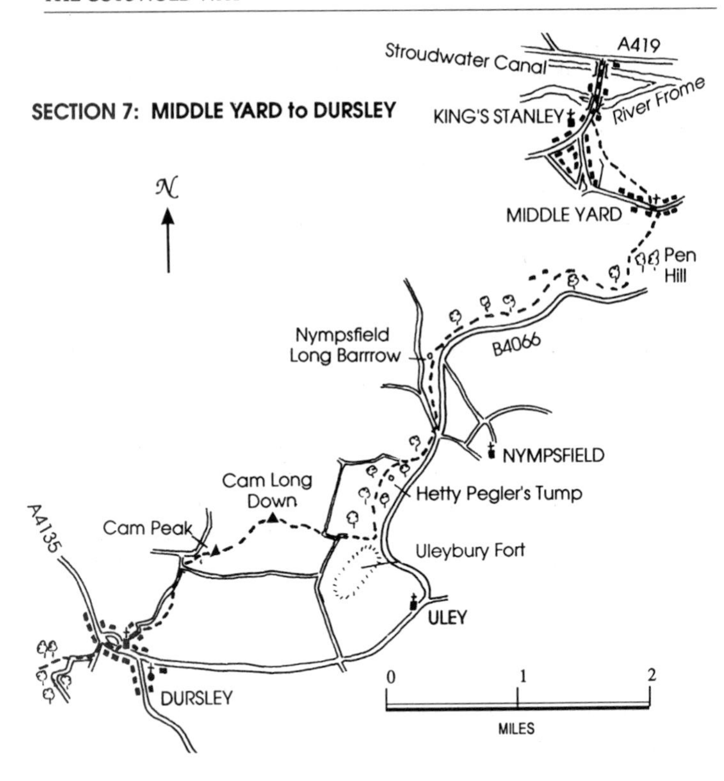

hillside field which you cross diagonally to its top right-hand corner. Go through a squeeze stile and bear left on a metalled lane, then up another enclosed path.

When you come to the edge of woods hugging Pen Hill bear right and continue, following a fence. The slope eases and you contour along the hillside on a lovely woodland path among tall, straight, green-trunked beeches looking so regal - wonderful in autumn. On a gentle descent a waymark suddenly directs you off the main path and onto a more narrow one cutting slightly uphill, but which loses height again shortly after.

Wander through the woods for some distance. Eventually the path

Wander through the woods for some distance. Eventually the path narrows and takes you through a rough area of coppice, into a jungly undergrowth and across a stile onto a grassy hillside above some barns. (Views ahead include the River Severn.)

Maintain direction across the slope, pass above Woodside Farm then, after hugging the woodland edge for a while, re-enter Stanley Woods by way of a stile. Continue straight ahead, rising gently, then through a wooden squeeze stile and over a crossing track. Go up a few steps and continue to gain height. After a while the woodland path eases to make a more gentle contour round the hillside; trees with just sufficient space between them to allow glimpsed views out to the right. The upper hillside eases and you discover that the path is running parallel with a road. Waymarks direct you along the fenced edge of a small wooded quarry, and soon after this you leave the woods and come out on an open grassy space near the car park for Coaley Peak Country Park *(Information, public toilets).*

From the car park go across the open meadow to find the Nympsfield long barrow (1) (Grid ref: 794015). Continue to the scarp edge of Frocester Hill with its magnificent views. Drawing the eye is flat-topped Cam Long Down off to the south-west. The escarpment sweeps in a great curve; the Severn winds along in the west, and down below farms appear little more than dolls' houses. A lovely viewpoint, worth giving time to absorb.

Wander along the scarp edge to a kissing gate at the far end of the grassland. Go through this and down the slope a little. Passing an exposed section of limestone cliff, the path then works its way up a series of wood-braced steps and comes to a road. Bear left. In a few paces you will come to the B4066 where you head to the right. A short distance along this a Cotswold Way signpost directs a bridlepath down into woodlands, soon very steeply. (**Note:** to visit Hetty Pegler's Tump (2) continue along the roadside for a further half mile.)

The Cotswold Way proper descends the scarp face very steeply, comes to a junction of five tracks, and then continues half-left ahead with the Way soon becoming a sunken track - extremely muddy in wet weather. This brings you to the head of a narrow lane on the edge of the woods (Grid ref: 790003), but you ignore this and instead bear left on a signposted footpath climbing uphill again into Coaley Wood. (Waymarks are rather sparse on this section.) The path forks and you bear left to climb a long series of steps. At the top of these the path levels out and becomes a belvedere with delightful views to enjoy. Eventually you come past an exposed quarried cliff and onto a broad crossing track near road-level at Crawley Barns. (**Note:** to visit Uleybury Hill Fort (3) simply go up a little further to the left. The ramparts of this ancient site make for an interesting circuit.)

To continue the route, cross the broad track and descend the bridleway opposite. It soon becomes embedded in a gully-like sunken track, then emerges at the foot of the slope between Springfield and Hodgecomb Farms. Go straight ahead on the track towards the obvious hillock of Cam Long Down.

The track veers left to a narrow country lane where you bear right for about 100 yards or so until coming to some barns. Cross a stile seen to the left of the barns and go straight ahead following the right-hand fence. A second stile takes you out of the field and onto the lower meadow slopes of Cam Long Down (4). Climb directly ahead up the slope to reach a pair of stiles under an ancient oak tree. Over these you soon wind among scrub and cramped trees to emerge onto the summit of the hill.

A wonderful panorama is to be had from here: the windings of the Severn, now a wide river of substance to the west with the Forest of Dean as backing, the curving Cotswold escarpment, the clustered streets of Dursley below to the south-west and Downham Hill, another flat-topped outlier, looking most attractive to the south. There are more tiny villages to the north, green meadows set out between hedgerow envelopes and an aura of peace and well-being.

Cross the ridge to its western end, then take the descending footpath to the saddle connecting Cam Long Down with Cam Peak (Peaked Down). Wander up to this secondary summit, where bracken threatens to engulf the complete hill, and you will find a curious metal construction on the top. More broad views are to be had from here, including the lofty Tyndale Monument beyond Dursley which will be visited on Section 8.

The descent to Dursley entails tackling a very steep slope of cropped turf which can be rather greasy under damp conditions when caution is advised. Descend to the right of a solitary house nestling at the base of the hill and continue down into a boggy corner of trees and bushes where you will find a gate taking you onto a narrow lane. Bear left and a few yards later, opposite Down House Farm, go over a stile and walk across a field to a second stile in a hedge leading to a road junction. Cross the road and walk straight ahead (signposted Dursley) for about 400 yards. A CW sign now directs you to the left, over a stile, then over another by a metal field gate where you bear right along a field boundary. Cross two or three small fields to the left of farm buildings, and make for the corner of a red-brick house where first a stile, then a kissing gate, put you down some steps and out to a driveway between houses and a bowling green. This will lead directly to Long Street, Dursley. Bear left to walk through Long Street among shops to reach the covered Market House in the centre of the town (5) *(Accommodation, refreshments, shops, post office etc.)* (Grid ref: 757981)

Things Seen on the Way:

(1) **Nympsfield Long Barrow** is similar in concept to many Neolithic barrows of the Severn-Cotswold Group. Built around 2800 BC it was used for burials and, probably, as a place of ritual. The site was first excavated in the 19th century when bones of 13 people, together with a flint arrowhead and some pottery, were discovered in the pair of side chambers that lead from the main passageway. The barrow has obviously deteriorated somewhat over the years, and the drystone walling is merely a reconstruction based on the original.

(2) **Hetty Pegler's Tump,** found about a mile to the south of Nympsfield Long Barrow, is another Neolithic burial mound and one in very good condition. It is 140 feet long by 90 feet wide, and the covering mound is about 10 feet high. From a long internal passageway there are two pairs of side chambers and a single chamber at the western end. The two northern chambers have been sealed off. 19th

Entrance chamber to Hetty Pegler's Tump

century excavations unearthed pieces of Roman pottery and an Edward IV silver groat. The mound (or tump) gained its curious name because it stands on land that was owned in the 17th century by Henry and Hester (or Hetty) Pegler. It is kept locked today in order to protect it from too much wear, but the key is available from a cottage at Crawley Barns.

(3) **Uleybury Hill Fort** occupies more than 30 acres of land on the very edge of the escaprment south-east of Cam Long Down. Built in the Iron Age it is certainly an impressive and well-chosen site as it has a 300 foot drop down the scarp face to help protect it. A ditch and rampart complete the defences. Uleybury has never been excavated, although 2nd and 4th century Roman coins have been picked up here.

(4) **Cam Long Down** came into being, according to legend, when the Devil decided to dam the River Severn and drown the people of Gloucestershire in revenge for their having built too many churches. Above Dursley he filled his wheelbarrow with a great chunk of the Cotswolds and was resting from his labours when along came a cobbler wearing a string of shoes to be mended draped around his neck. When the Devil asked for directions to the river, the suspicious cobbler explained that it was so far that he had already worn out several pairs of shoes on the way from it. The Devil lost heart and emptied his load. The wheelbarrow-load of stone, of course, was Cam Long Down. (Similar folk legends occur all over the country.) Strip lynchets may be seen on the south-facing slopes, while the summit plateau is broken with strange undulations which might indicate the existence of some form of ancient settlement.

(5) **Dursley** was once one of the principal wool and cloth towns of the Cotswolds, but with the decline in woollen manufacture it made a remarkable transition to modern engineering. Transition seems to be in the blood of the town, for Roger Berkeley, cousin to Edward the Confessor, held the manor of Dursley and had built himself a castle (long since disappeared) when the Normans landed, but rather than be replaced by a favourite of the invaders, he was allowed to retain his position. Eventually manorial ties were severed

and the new masters were those whose power came from wool. Now, as elsewhere along the Cotswolds, the dependence on sheep is but a memory, but the town survives in its own right, although the price has been the substitution of a number of old buildings by others of less architectural merit. The Market House, built in 1738, remains as model of a past era. There is a bell turret and a niche with a statue depicting Queen Anne facing the church.

* * *

SECTION 8: DURSLEY TO WOTTON-UNDER-EDGE

Distance:	7 miles.
Map:	O.S. Landranger series; Sheet 162 (Gloucester & Forest of Dean Area), 1:50,000.
Accommodation:	North Nibley - b&b, camping. Wotton-under-Edge - b&b, camping three quarters of a mile off-route.

The Way continues to explore the western edge of the escarpment with its wide vistas that include the River Severn and Forest of Dean. There is a section of low-lying farmland to cross, and this is as interesting in its way as the scarp edge. By contrast with the previous walk, on this stage there is only one prehistoric site - the hill fort of Brackenbury Ditches to the south of the lofty Tyndale Monument (built to record the life of William Tyndale who translated the Bible into English).

From Dursley a steep climb through woodland leads onto Stinchcombe Hill. A circuit of the plateau is made in order to capture one of the finest of all Cotswold panoramas, then follows a descent over an agricultural landscape to the little village of North Nibley. Another climb takes you back to the escarpment by the Tyndale Monument on Nibley Knoll, through Westridge Woods and past Brackenbury Ditches. Wotton Hill comes next, with its circular enclosure of the Jubilee Plantation, from which a splendid view looks over Wotton-under-Edge. The path down into this old wool town is in itself rather interesting and makes a fitting conclusion to the day.

Refreshments are available in North Nibley.

* * *

To leave Dursley walk through the pedestrian shopping precinct behind the old Market House, and at the far end go left into May Lane. Follow this until Hill Road branches from it, then walk up Hill Road until it swings to the left. At this point leave the road to climb ahead on a steep woodland path the middle of three, which leads directly onto Stinchcombe Hill (1). You emerge from the woods by the golf club-house to begin a tour of the upper plateau. At present waymarking is barely adequate and concentration is required. But

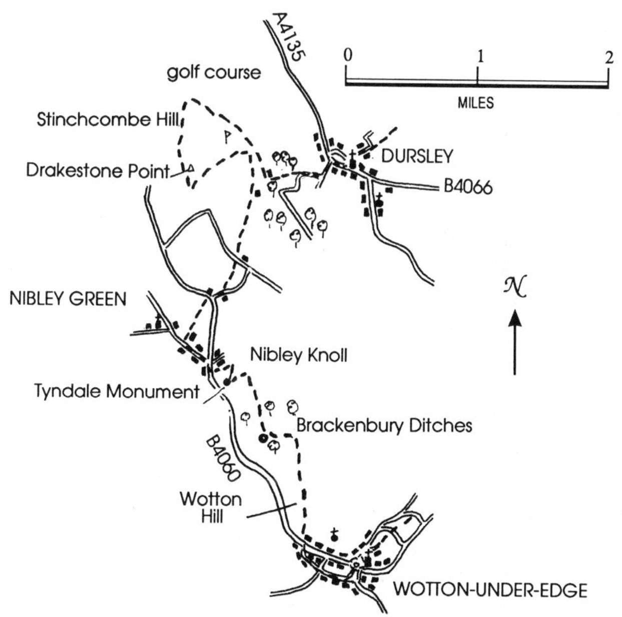

SECTION 8: DURSLEY to WOTTON-UNDER-EDGE

views from the edges are magnificent, especially from a shelter dedicated to the memory of the former owner of this land, Sir Stanley William Tubbs, and from the highest part of the hill, Drakestone Point, where there is a topograph.

The tour of Stinchcombe Hill begins by going left from the club-house, then right on a narrow road across the golf course. Just beyond a small parking area go half-left across fairways to the left-hand end of a woodland. Continue ahead, but as the path goes into woods turn sharp left across a tee where a trail leads into the upper edge of woods hanging on the scarp slope. The path curves leftwards, passes the Tubbs shelter and continues to the topograph and promontory seat on Drakestone Point. Return a few paces from the seat and veer right on another path descending a little. It cuts across the steep scarp slope and eventually leads to the car parking area seen earlier. Near the end of the golf course a waymark directs you into woods on the right for a steep descent of the hillside.

Near the foot of the slope leave the bridleway for a path on the left near gas pipes. The way now crosses sloping fields to a stile leading onto a narrow lane by Park Farm House (Grid ref: 744972).
Turn left, and a few paces later cross a stile on your right into a large field. A signpost here directs the route to North Nibley. Walk through the middle of the field and out by way of another stile on the far side, then straight ahead to the edge of a steep slope. The continuing path goes half-right, crosses yet another stile and comes out onto a lane by some cottages. Bear right and follow the lane round to a road junction.

Cross straight ahead onto a bridleway heading among trees. Along this trackway you will pass an old doorway dated 1607 in the right-hand wall, of which little appears to be known. The Way narrows to become almost a tunnel, then emerges to a lane in front of some houses. Continue straight ahead, then bear left into The Street, North Nibley (2) *(Accommodation, refreshments, shop)* (Grid ref: 740958).

The Street leads to the B4060 opposite The Black Horse Inn. Turn right and walk alongside the road as far as a public telephone kiosk, then cross to the left-hand side where the Cotswold Way continues

The Jubilee Plantation on Wotton Hill

as a classic sunken track going up to Nibley Knoll and the Tyndale Monument. (The monument is kept locked, but if you wish to climb it to the top, note the location of the key which is given on a notice-board at the foot of the track.) Near the top of the track break away to the right on another path which curves round to a set of bars, then onto a hilltop meadow dominated by the tall grey tower, solemn-looking with its iron railings round the base and a cross on top (3). A nearby topograph highlights major items in the huge view, including the Severn Bridge, 12 miles away, and Haresfield Beacon (visited on Section 6, now 10 miles distant as the crow flies, but no less than 18 along the Cotswold Way).

Go to the monument, then back along the scarp edge to find the entrance to Westridge Wood. Inside the wood are numerous crossing tracks and side paths, but at each junction there are waymarks to guide you. On the route through you will pass the site of Brackenbury Ditches (4). The path comes out of the wood and continues alongside it, following the right-hand boundary of a large field. At the top corner of the field a stile takes the path into a small promontory meadow (Wotton Hill) on which stool-ball was played during the reign of Edward I. The hill is marked by a clump of commemorative trees set within a circular wall (5). From it there are fine views overlooking Wotton-under-Edge.

The steep descending path drops down the forward left-hand slope of this promontory meadow. A waymark post directs from below, and on the way to it care should be exercised, especially should the grass be damp.

A stile and a set of steps lead onto a lane. Go straight across and down the continuing footpath which brings you to a road leading left into Wotton (6) *(Accommodation, refreshments, shops, post office etc.).* Take the first road junction on the right (Bradley Street) to High Street, which in turn comes to Long Street with shops on either side. Bear left into Church Street, then right at the bottom to take a raised footpath leading to an alleyway called The Cloud. This leads to a crossing alleyway (Shinbone Alley) where you turn left and wander up to the churchyard of the handsome Parish Church of St Mary the Virgin (Grid ref: 760935).

Things Seen on the Way:

(1) **Stinchcombe Hill** above Dursley was given to the public by Sir Stanley Tubbs. It is a magnificent viewpoint, with the eye being drawn to Berkeley Castle and the nuclear power station beyond it. The Malvern Hills, Brecon Beacons and even, so it is claimed, Exmoor, can be seen from here.

(2) **North Nibley** is 'the clearing near the peak'. Among its 18th century dwellings is Nibley House, partially rebuilt in 1763 from an earlier house. The church is rather fine and dates from the 15th century. Nearby is Nibley Green where the last battle to be fought in England between private armies took place in 1470 between the Berkeleys and the Lisles. About 2,000 men took part and Lord Lisle, who had challenged Lord Berkeley to do battle, was shot first in the face then stabbed to death. His retainer army fled and was scattered over the surrounding countryside, while his house was sacked by Berkeley's men. Around 150 men died in the senseless battle.

(3) **The Tyndale Monument** on Nibley Knoll is an impressive and prominent landmark, 111 feet high and designed by S.S. Teulon. It

was erected in 1866 in memory of William Tyndale who translated the Bible into English. Whilst a plaque here suggests he was born at North Nibley, this is now suspected to be wrong. Apparently a Tyndale did live nearby at about the right time, but he was not even related to the William Tyndale who was martyred in Flanders on October 6th, 1536.

(4) **Brackenbury Ditches** is the name given to another Iron Age hill fort, rather overgrown with trees, but not entirely hidden. The outer defensive ditch has been cleared, but presumably because of the dense woodland cover within, the site has never been excavated. Nearby in Westridge Wood is the site of an outlawed cockpit.

(5) **The Jubilee Plantation** on Wotton Hill was planted initially to celebrate the victory against Napoleon at Waterloo in 1815, but in order to mark the end of the Crimean War the trees were felled for a bonfire. The circular wall was erected and more trees planted in 1887 to celebrate Queen Victoria's jubilee. Again new planting took place in 1952.

(6) **Wotton-under-Edge** was first mentioned in a royal charter dated 940 AD - its Saxon name means 'the farm in the wood'. The original village was almost completely destroyed by fire during the reign of King John as a reprisal for Lord Berkeley's part in the lead up to Magna Carta. The rebuilt town achieved the status of a borough in 1253 and grew to become an important wool town with several productive mills situated along the stream that runs through it. The Parish Church of St Mary the Virgin is a real gem. Dating from 1283 it is said to replace one that was destroyed during the earlier burning of the town. Katherine, Lady Berkeley, has a fine brass. It was she who gave Wotton the distinction of the first school founded by a woman (in 1384). Isaac Pitman, who developed his shorthand system here, was the first master at another Wotton school, the British School on the corner of Bear Lane. The oldest house in the town is said to be the former Ram Inn (1350, to the south of the church), while the 17th century gabled almshouses in Church Street, built through a bequest by Hugh Perry, have within their courtyard a lovely chapel containing some splendid stained glass. All in all the town is a pleasing mixture of past and present, tucked against the wooded wolds.

SECTION 9: WOTTON-UNDER-EDGE TO HAWKESBURY UPTON

Distance:	8 miles.
Map:	O.S. Landranger series; Sheet 172 (Bristol, Bath & Surrounding Area), 1:50,000.
Accommodation:	Wortley - b&b (half a mile off-route). Hillesley - b&b, (three-quarters of a mile off-route). Hawkesbury Upton - b&b.

On this stage of the walk one is reminded yet again of the district's past dependence on the wool and cloth industries, for in places the route leads through valleys and alongside streams whose power was formerly harnessed by cloth mills. Some of these mills are still to be seen along the Way. Others which once lined the valleys disappeared with the coming of the Industrial Revolution. Though many of the mills have gone, the valleys and their streams remain to give the walker a day of gentle pleasures. But in spite of these valley sections the path does not completely desert the high wolds, for it is not long after leaving Wotton that the escarpment is gained once more. Yet again there are woodlands for company, and deep-cut sunken tracks to follow. More charming, typical Cotswold cottages adorn the lower slopes and there's plenty of variety to maintain interest all the way.

As the Cotswold crow flies, Hawkesbury Upton is barely 4 miles from Wotton, but the route doubles that distance without difficulty on its zig-zag course along the scarp edge and in and out of 'back-country' valleys. On this stage you pass out of Gloucestershire at last and enter the county of Avon.

From Wotton-under-Edge the route leads initially north-eastwards alongside a lovely stream towards Coombe, then south and east steeply up Blackquarries Hill with views growing in extent once more. Head round Wortley Hill and Tor Hill, among woods, then down a deep track to the edge of Wortley village. A cross-country section of agricultural land takes the Way to tiny Alderley before following the millstream of Kilcott Brook through a lovely peaceful vale, then up to the Somerset Monument on the outskirts of Hawkesbury Upton. This is a pleasant walk, during which the very nature of the Cotswold Way begins to change.

* * *

On leaving the churchyard of St Mary the Virgin turn right and walk along the street to Valley Road which breaks away to the right. This curves to the left and brings you to a stream - a clear, chuckling, friendly companion to follow for a while. A footpath leads alongside the stream, across a narrow lane coming from Holywell, and continues in the same direction to Coombe. On reaching a second narrow lane turn right and walk along it, but by the side of a house called The Hive leave the roadway and turn left on a bridleway rising steeply among trees. Still climbing, you will come to a lane where you turn left onto Blackquarries Hill.

Out of tree-shade the lane runs along the hilltop between fields. Follow this for a little over half a mile, but a few paces after coming to a strip of woodland on the left a track cuts sharply back to the right with a signpost indicating the way to Tor Hill, Wortley and Alderley. Head along this track beside a drystone wall. Views from here take in the Tyndale Monument to the north-west across Wotton's valley, and far beyond that to a succession of curving spurs and indents of the scarp.

The track turns into a field on the left. Ignore this and continue straight ahead through a field gate to follow a crumbling wall. The wall finishes and has a wire fence continuing. About 80 yards beyond the wall, go through a field gate on the left and follow a faint path across the sloping terrace of hillside with the scarp edge plunging steeply away to the right. This is one of the last edges of the walk.

On the far side of the terrace go through a narrow strip of woodland, then bear right along a track. It begins to lose height and cuts into a plantation. Several alternative tracks break away, but waymarks keep you ahead on course. When the main track skirts left, continue straight ahead on a narrow path among woods. The path becomes a deeply sunken track with steep banks draped with ivy and

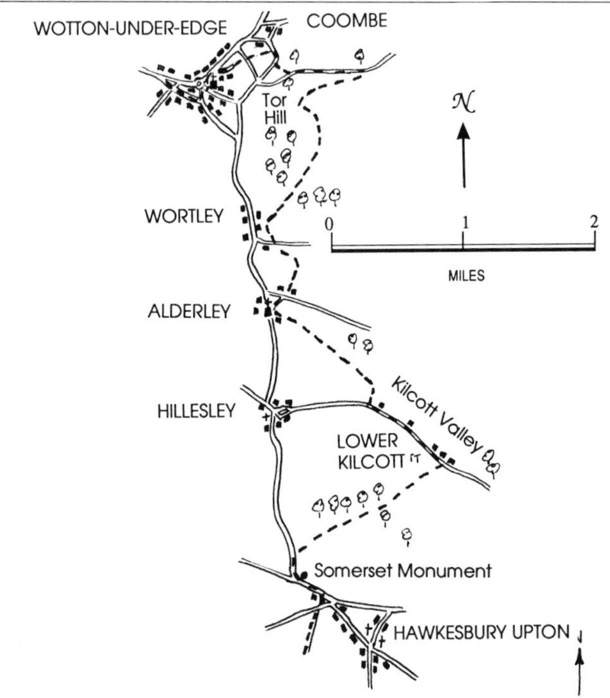

SECTION 9: WOTTON-UNDER-EDGE to HAWKESBURY UPTON

hart's tongue fern, with trees high overhead to complete the tunnel effect. This is a splendid section, full of charm and an unquiet mystery.

Eventually you emerge onto a farm track where you head left. This leads to a lane on the outskirts of Wortley (1) *(Accommodation)*. Instead of going into the village cross a stile and go half-left over a field, directed by a large yellow arrow seen on a pole carrying power cables on the far side of the field. A stile near some willows leads into a smaller field, and over this another stile will be found by a field gate. Cross a stream coming out of a valley (known as Ozleworth Bottom) onto a track that curves to the right into Kennerwell Lane and brings you to Alderley, a charming little village worth giving a few minutes to explore (2).

Cross the road straight ahead and keep on to another junction near the church. Bear left in front of a house onto a drive that leads to a farm track. Through a field gate the track now descends south-eastwards into the very pleasant Kilcott valley.

The route heads into the valley without difficulty. Simply maintain direction along the right-hand boundary of several meadows linked one to another by gates or stiles. The path which replaces the farm track takes you into a brambly corner, through a metal gate and along a narrow enclosed section. This brings you to a farm track/green lane, often very wet, where you turn right, crossing out of Gloucestershire and into Avon. About 200 yards along this you cross the Kilcott Brook and come to a country road where you head to the left (Grid ref: 779898). (**Note**: for accommodation or refreshments turn right on this road and walk to Hillesley, about three-quarters of a mile away.)

Having turned left walk along the road, the Kilcott Brook washing alongside for company, and before long you will pass Kilcott Mill looking most attractive with its pond and old stone buildings on your left. Three-quarters of a mile after joining the road you come to the few cottages that comprise the hamlet of Lower Kilcott. A sunken track here breaks away to the right, signposted to Hawkesbury Monument and Hawkesbury.

The track is a bridleway, so do not be surprised to find it rather muddy. It rises gently and passes through a field gate. Bear right, then follow a hedge on your left. At the far end a stile is found next to a metal field gate. This takes you into a woodland on a sometimes muddy path. Before long the path-cum-track divides. The bridleway goes to the right while the footpath route continues ahead (they combine again later). Continue through the wood, then along its left-hand edge, and come to a gate with a large field beyond.

Walk ahead through the field aiming just to the right of a large dutch barn seen in the distance. Come to a metal field gate leading onto a road near the barn. Bear left and walk alongside the road towards the lofty Somerset (or Hawkesbury) Monument (3). Continue past the monument on the road to Hawkesbury Upton. The Cotswold Way does not go right into the village itself, but turns off to the right by a pond shortly after passing the village sign (Grid ref: 775874). (**Note:** for accommodation, refreshments, shop and post office, continue along the road 400 yards beyond the CW turn-off to reach the centre of Hawkesbury Upton (4).)

Things Seen on the Way:

(1) **Wortley** is only a short road distance to the south of Wotton-under-Edge, but is reached by a devious footpath route. The village was heavily involved in the district's cloth trade by virtue of the number of mills in the neighbourhood that were powered by local streams. It is also famed as being the birthplace of Stephen Hopkins who made his fortune in that cloth trade and then sailed to America in the *Mayflower* in 1620 with the Pilgrim Fathers. There he became an important official and died in 1644.

(2) **Alderley** is 'the clearing in the alders'. A small yet charming hamlet on a splay of country roads midway between Wortley and Hillesley, set on a spur of land between the Ozleworth and Kilcott valleys. Here lived a Lord Chief Justice, Matthew Hale (1609-76); a botanical artist, Marianne North (died 1890); and another eminent botanist, Brian Houghton Hodgson, who lived for a while at The Grange. But long before all these, in the 13th century, one Alderley inhabitant claimed himself to be Jesus Christ, whereupon he was sent by the magistrates to Oxford for execution. Some say he died by crucifixion.

(3 **The Somerset Monument** just outside Hawkesbury Upton dates from 1846. It was erected in memory of General Lord Robert Edward Henry Somerset, a son of the 5th Duke of Beaufort whose family seat was at nearby Badminton (of horse trials fame). General Somerset served under Wellington at the Battle of Waterloo, but whether this was commendable enough in itself to warrant such a lofty memorial is questionable. It stands more than 120 feet high and for a small fee you can climb the 144 steps to the viewing platform.

(4) **Hawkesbury Upton** grew around a farm mentioned in a document of 972 AD but has grown very little since then in its thousand-year history. In fact its expansion has been surprisingly limited despite its prominent position on the wolds just west of the Bath road, and most of the village is less than a hundred years old.

* * *

SECTION 10: HAWKESBURY UPTON TO TORMARTON

Distance:	8 miles.
Map:	O.S. Landranger series; Sheet 172 (Bristol, Bath & Surrounding Area), 1:50,000.
Accommodation:	Horton - b&b (three-quarters of a mile off-route). Old Sodbury - hotel, b&b. Tormarton - b&b.

Although there are 3 or 4 small villages along this section of the route, it is very much a peaceful, seemingly remote stretch of countryside to wander through, and whilst it has none of the previous scarp edge vastness of view, there are nevertheless distant vistas of great beauty to enjoy. The descent to Horton Court is a highlight, so is the visit to Sodbury hill fort and the crossing of Dodington Park.

Within a few yards of rejoining the route by the pond in Hawkesbury Upton, the Way follows along an old green lane called Bath Lane. I once found this to be an apt name when walking through one day, for it was badly waterlogged from days of heavy autumnal rain and I waded through with no opportunity to dodge it, the water coming well above the top of my walking boots! (The name of the lane, of course, actually refers to the town of Bath at the end of an old trading route, of which this was but a section.) The approach to Horton Court, coming off the hills near the end of Bath Lane, presents a broad panorama over the low-lying land to the west, while from Horton to Little Sodbury you walk through a 'lost' farmland dotted with sheep. Lanes and more field paths take the Way from Little Sodbury to Old Sodbury, then on to graceful, pheasant-scurrying Dodington Park. Tormarton at the end of this stage shyly tries to hide itself away from the busy A46, which makes a by-pass to the west, and the deep cut of the M4 to the south. Here it seems, the Cotswolds have been lost and all but forgotten.

Refreshments are available in Old Sodbury.

* * *

The village pond in Hawkesbury Upton is set in a triangle of roads. As you approach it from the Somerset Monument turn right, then shortly after go left on a bridleway track signposted to Horton 3.5 kilometres. This is Bath Lane, which you follow to its end. Do not go onto the road (Highfield Lane) which crosses it, but bear right on a footpath that runs parallel to the road, along the left-hand edge of two fields. On entering the third field, with a stone barn ahead, bear half-right, pass a group of trees and bushes near the barn, go through a gap in the hedgerow and ahead along the edge of a large field. After about 100 yards veer right above a hollow where the way is guided by marker posts to the lower edge of a field. Before long cross a stile into woods and continue along the hillslope among fine trees (mostly beech) and with enticing views between them down onto Horton's church. The path goes down a few steps, then swings to the right and continues downhill to the edge of the beechwood which you leave by way of a field gate. Head down a sloping meadow to a lane near Horton Court (1).

Turn left and wander along the lane which is lined here and there with holm oak, with fine views off to the right to set you dreaming as you approach the village of Horton. Just before coming to a minor road junction by the village school, you pass by an Iron Age hill fort above you to the left (Grid ref: 764843) *(Accommodation in Horton).*

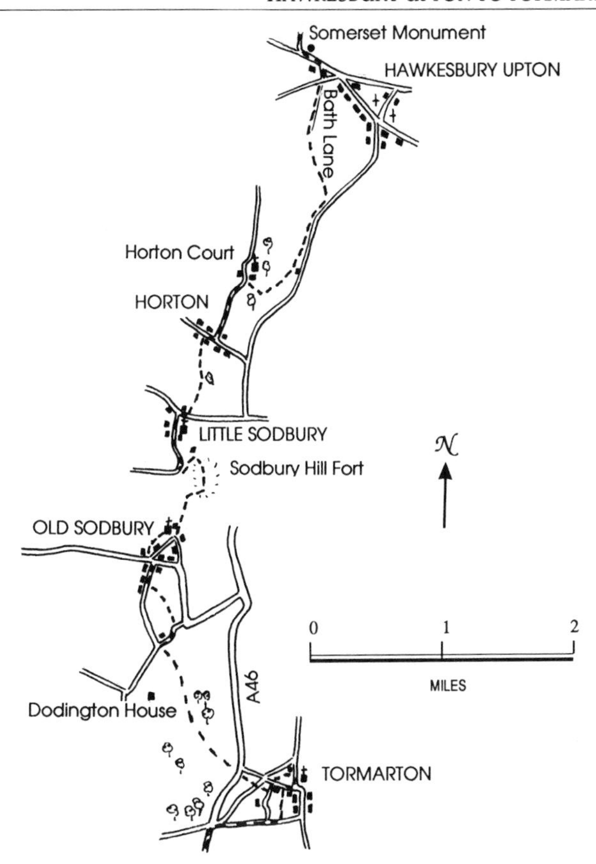

SECTION 10: HAWKESBURY UPTON to TORMARTON

At the junction bear right, and a few yards later go left on a drive with a signpost to Little Sodbury. A footpath leads from the drive and you cross through the middle of a field to a stile on the far side, then steeply down into a dip with a farm reservoir, formed by the damming of a stream, seen to the left. Go up the opposite slope and into the next field where you follow the right-hand boundary.

Maintain direction through subsequent fields towards a cottage. The footpath leads alongside this and comes out on a road opposite Little Sodbury church, dedicated to St Adeline, its squat tower half-hidden among yew and beech trees (2). For such a small place Little Sodbury holds a remarkable place in English history.

The church stands at a road junction. Turn right, then left onto the road signposted to Old Sodbury, passing first the church, then The Laurels and, on the right, the well scrubbed Church Farm. Continue along the road until a drive breaks away left to the Manor House. Turn left along this and almost immediately branch right on an enclosed footpath. Through a gate head left up the slope, then go sharp right in front of some farm buildings to find a stile by a gate leading onto Sodbury hill fort (3).

Waymarks lead through the northern ramparts and across the shallow rectangular centre of the fort, then out through the earth ramparts on the southern side. A footpath goes into a small woodland and down a slope. Once out of the trees go left over a stile and walk ahead along the lower right-hand boundary of a field. On the far side of this go over another stile in the corner and pass to the left of Hayes Farm onto an enclosed path which brings you out by the village school in Old Sodbury.

Walk through the churchyard of the stumpy-towered church of St John the Baptist (the tower is original 13th century) and out the far side through a metal kissing gate into a sloping meadow. Leave this by a stile in the bottom left-hand corner, beyond which you continue towards a black barn with another stile to the left of it. Walk through the farmyard to the main A432 road opposite The Dog Inn in Old Sodbury (Grid ref: 754816) *(Accommodation, refreshments, shop).*

Cross the A432 and walk ahead along Chapel Lane for about 400 yards, then take a footpath to the left through a gate and go half-right across fields (passing to the left of a small pond) and out at the far right corner. Once over a stile maintain direction and climb the hillslope, pass through a gap in a hedge and continue along the right-hand side of dividing hedges, making to the left of some cottages.

Coming onto a country road turn right to Coombes End. Shortly

The Cotswold Way below Haresfield Beacon (Section 6)

after passing a road junction the Cotswold Way continues by way of a stile on the left, with a signpost to Tormarton. Walk across a field passing to the right of a raised group of trees, and on the far side cross a pair of stiles and a long tarmac drive (leading to Dodington House (4), unseen off to the right). The Way continues through the parkland, busy with pheasant and guinea fowl. By a metal field gate there is a novel squeeze stile, and through this you must go half-left and by way of stiles maintain this direction across Dodington Park, climbing a steep slope and at the top climbing over another stile next to a field gate. Now bear half-left and wander along a woodland edge with fine views ahead of a gentle, wooded, comfortable landscape.

When the woodland branches back to the left, continue straight ahead and down an easy sloping field. Near the bottom cross a stile and a footbridge over a stream (the beginnings of the River Frome which flows into the Avon in Bristol), then walk up to the left-hand end of a strip of woodland. The path leads up to the busy A46 which has been crossed and recrossed several times since it was first met in Broadway on Section 1.

Cross the road with the utmost caution. The continuing path is signposted to Tormarton and begins next to an old milestone half-hidden on the verge. Across the field, go over a narrow road and continue straight ahead through the next field with a second lane beyond. Maintain direction through a third field towards a row of houses, but on joining a road bear left and a few paces later turn right and cross a field towards the church of St Mary Magdalene. Bear right on a road in front of the church. On coming to a road junction turn right in front of The Portcullis Inn, then immediately beyond the pub go left along a driveway to leave Tormarton (5) (Grid ref: 768788) *(Accommodation, refreshments).*

Things Seen on the Way:

(1) **Horton Court** must be one of the oldest inhabited houses in England, for parts in use today were built in 1140, not eighty years after the Normans arrived. The house, owned by the National Trust and open to the public on set days between April and October, is part

Springtime path in Alderley (Section 9)

An old milestone by the side of the Cotswold Way, on the outskirts of Tormarton

Norman, part Tudor Gothic in a splendid setting near the church. The manor was originally in the hands of a son of King Harold, but was confiscated and given to Robert de Tedini. The hall is all that remains of the original construction, but the roof is 14th century. In 1521 the main part of the house was built for William Knight, chief secretary to Henry VIII and an eminent churchman who was sent to Rome in an attempt to persuade the Pope to annul Henry's marriage to Catherine of Aragon. The attempt was unsuccessful, but Knight had seen much to interest him in Italy and his attraction to the architecture of Rome was later to be expressed in parts of Horton Court.

(2) **Little Sodbury** is a tiny hamlet with a manor built in 1486 for Sir John Walsh. In 1521 William Tyndale came to Little Sodbury as chaplain to Sir John's household. Here he began translating into English Erasmus's *Enchiridion Militis Christiani* and preaching in

what was then seen to be an outspoken manner. One oft quoted incident occurred here: when at dinner one evening at the manor, a visiting dignitary protested at Tyndale's views with the remark "We were better be without God's law than the Pope's." Tyndale was defiant - "I defy the Pope and all his laws. If God shall spare my life, ere many years I will cause the boy that follows the plough to know more of the Bible than thou doest." He left Little Sodbury for London in 1523, then travelled to the continent where he met Miles Coverdale. In 1526 Tyndale's English version of the New Testament was published at Worms (the Old Testament followed in 1530), and ten years later he was put to death. The Parish Church of St Adeline, in which Tyndale preached, originally stood behind the manor but was demolished in 1859 and the present church built from some of the stones.

(3) **Sodbury Hill Fort** is one of the most impressive on the walk. Consisting of 11 acres enclosed by ramparts and ditches, it was constructed in the Iron Age but considerably strengthened by the Romans who, it is thought, used it as a frontier post. Although never excavated, a few Roman coins have been found in the turf. The Saxon army camped in the shelter of the ramparts in 577 AD, and in 1471 Edward IV rested here with his army on the way to do battle with Margaret of Anjou at Tewkesbury.

(4) **Dodington House and Park** are situated between Old Sodbury and Tormarton. The house is unseen from the Cotswold Way, although it is only a short distance from the path. In a secretive site it stands, a severe mansion (one of the largest of all in the Cotswolds) built on the site of a former Tudor house by James Wyatt in 1795 for Christopher Bethell Codrington, a man whose great wealth was made on the backs of slaves in the West Indies. The rolling parkland was landscaped by Capability Brown 30 years before the house was built, and it is this which gives the Cotswold Way walker an interlude of grace and the company of game birds scurrying to and fro.

(5) **Tormarton** is explored in a part circuit by the route which makes a dog-leg to visit the church of St Mary Magdalene which has gargoyles, some fine brasses and an interesting Jacobean pulpit. The

church is Norman, although it is thought a previous place of worship stood here in Saxon times. In those days the village stood at the borders of Wessex and Mercia, but nowadays the county boundaries of Wiltshire and Avon are just a short distance away to the east.

* * *

SECTION 11: TORMARTON TO COLD ASHTON

Distance:	6 miles.
Map:	O.S Landranger series; Sheet 172 (Bristol, Bath & Surrounding Area), 1:50,000.
Accommodation:	Cold Ashton - b&b.
	Nimlett - b&b, camping three-quarters of a mile off-route, south of Cold Ashton).

This very short penultimate stage of the long walk from Chipping Campden is given in order to highlight the possibility of overnight accommodation before tackling the final 10 mile stretch to Bath. It is an easy stage with few hills to wander across, but there's more road walking to contend with than on any other comparable section. This is not to suggest it is without interest, for the middle part of the walk has Dyrham (and a journey round the perimeter of the 246 acres of Dyrham Park) as a highlight, and it is near here that a return is made once more to the Cotswold scarp line.

Between Tormarton and Cold Asthon the Way crosses and recrosses the A46 and goes over the deep cut of the M4 motorway. A belt of woodland, followed by a skirting of several large fields, restores the countryside aspect of the walk. Then a country lane takes you to the edge of the extensive deer park that surrounds Dyrham House. Ancient field systems (strip lynchets) are seen on the slopes of Hinton Hill, and you gaze across a folding landscape towards Bristol which sprawls out in the west. The footpath leads to the edge of lovely, mellow Dyrham, past the gates of Dyrham House and into fields again on the cross-country route to Cold Ashton, a small village with a marvellous southerly aspect.

Refreshments are available in Pennsylvania, three-quarters of a mile before reaching Cold Ashton, and on the edge of Cold Ashton itself.

* * *

Having turned out of the street in Tormarton next to The Portcullis Inn, follow a footpath across a field, then over a stone stile and alongside the left-hand boundary of a second field. Round two sides of this you will find another stone stile which takes you onto a road, and here you must head to the right. On coming to a junction go left along the grass verge to reach the A46. Go left beside this busy road, then with great care negotiate the large roundabout which feeds traffic onto the M4 deep in its cutting beneath and continue along the grass verge of the A46 heading south-west towards Bath.

Keep along this road for about a third of a mile. Turn right on a tarmac footpath leading into a car park and picnic area *(public toilets)*, and continue ahead through a narrow strip of woodland. Out of this turn left, follow the field boundary beside the continuing woods and you will soon gain the first real view of folding hillsides and neat meadows for some time - a welcome return to countryside sanity after the traffic madness of minutes earlier.

When the woods finish continue along the field boundary, but near the bottom of this a waymark directs the path left into a new field. Walk alongside its right-hand hedgerow and maintain direction on a die-straight level course, passing beneath high-voltage power cables as you do, to come to a country road by a T-junction (Grid ref: 746769).

Take the forward road to maintain direction, heading towards some barns on the edge of Dyrham Park (1), but immediately before reaching these turn right along a bridleway (signposted to Dyrham) and follow the fine grey wall which contains the unseen deer park. As you walk alongside the wall note the clear evidence of ancient agriculture in the low banks of former terracing known as strip

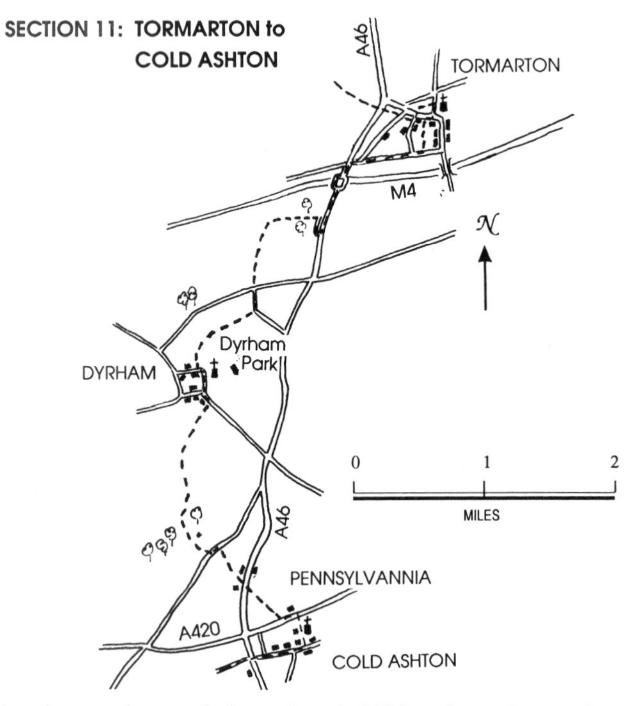

lynchets, and mounded remains of a hill fort above them to the north marked by a woodland - an historic site (2). Lovely panoramic views produce a tranquil scene all along this part of the walk.

Having wandered round the outside of Dyrham Park, pass through a metal field gate onto a sunken track which takes you down to the modest little village of Dyrham with its mellow stone cottages and bower of trees. Turn left and walk along the village street, passing the church entrance on your left, closely followed by a set of gates through which can be seen the west side of Dyrham House (now owned by the National Trust and open to the public most days from April to October).

Shortly after passing the gates you come to a minor road junction.

Bear left to rise out of the village, and when you come to the village sign leave the road and head to the right on a signposted footpath (Pennsylvania 2 kilometres, Cold Ashton 3 kilometres). Walk ahead along the right-hand boundary of a field, then cross a stile into a neighbouring field.

Maintain direction along a series of fields linked by more stiles. After duckboards take you over a boggy patch, you pass a pond and rise through the centre of a field. Go through a hedgerow gap and resume along the left-hand edge of the next large field. Over the brow of a hill the boundary hedge cuts off to the left, and at this point you leave it and continue ahead, maintaining direction but now sloping downhill towards woods.

A plank footbridge takes you over a stream, then through a woodland shaw and across the lower corner of the next field. Now wander uphill with a woodland on your left to find a stile taking you in among the trees on a path winding uphill through them. When you emerge, walk along the left-hand boundary of a hilltop field. At the far side you will come onto a road. Bear left for about 80 yards, then head to the right along a bridleway going to Pennsylvania.

Pennsylvania is a small hamlet astride the A46 (Grid ref: 744733) *(Refreshments)*. Cross the road with due caution to find a stile on the opposite side leading into the corner of a field. Cross this field to its top right-hand corner, go over another stile and maintain direction through this second field to the far left-hand corner where you exit onto the A420. Turn left towards The White Hart *(Refreshments)*, almost directly opposite the pub follow a footpath alongside a driveway to Cold Ashton's church (Grid ref: 751727). Walk through the churchyard, and on emerging from its south side bear right in Cold Ashton village street to pass several handsome buildings gazing out over a broad and undulating landscape (3) *(Accommodation, refreshments)*.

Things Seen on the Way:

(1) **Dyrham Park** is open throughout the year. It consists of 264 acres

Cold Ashton Manor

of deer-grazed grassland. These grounds, which surround the imposing Dyrham House, were formerly terraced and landscaped with magnificent water gardens featuring a great water spout and a cascade pouring over a series of more than 200 steps. The house itself, built for William III's Secretary of War - William Blathwayt - is in fact 2 houses standing back-to-back to replace an original Tudor mansion. The older of these two houses was built at the end of the 17th century, the other about six years later (finished around 1704). The herd of fallow deer roaming the parkland is reckoned to be one of the oldest in the country.

(2) **Hinton Hill Fort** is also known as Dyrham (or Burrill) Camp. On this site in 577 AD an historic and decisive battle was fought between the Saxons and the ancient Britons, the outcome giving control of Gloucester, Cirencester and Bath to the Saxons, the Britons being driven back to Wales and Somerset. An Anglo-Saxon chronicle

records the event in concise terms:

"Cuthwine and Cealwin fought against the Brytwalas. They slew three kings, Coinmail, Condidan and Farinmail, at the place called Dyrham, and captured three cities ..."

In many ways this battle set the course of English history by re-drawing political and cultural boundaries

(3) **Cold Ashton** deserves its prefix by virtue of the winds which sweep in off the Bristol Channel to catch its exposed face. But it is a charming place for all that, on the southern edge of the Cotswold plateau with fine views that overlook land on which medieval farmers grew vines. The gabled Elizabethan Manor, with its tall chimneys and ornate gateway, stands next door to the rectory and partially hidden from the Cotswold wayfarer by walls and clipped yew hedges. It is considered by some to be one of the finest examples of this type of building in the country.

* * *

SECTION 12: COLD ASHTON TO BATH

Distance:	10 miles.
Map:	O.S. Landranger series; Sheet 172 (Bristol, Bath & Surrounding Area), 1:50,000.
Accommodation:	Weston - guest-house. Bath - hotels, guest-houses, b&b, youth hostel.

There are many pleasures to be gained on this walk; some fine broad panoramas, a varied landscape of hill and dale, of intimate scenarios and one of the loveliest vistas to be sampled anywhere along the Cotswolds just before the final downhill swoop to Bath. Then, of course, there's the architectural climax of Bath itself, best enjoyed perhaps on a late afternoon as the low sun picks out the texture of the town's graceful streets glowing in the westerly light. The final tramp along Union Passage, turning at last to be confronted by the magnificent abbey ahead and the ancient Roman baths to one side, makes the ultimate climax to a long walk - a most memorable conclusion to a memorable journey.

Out of Cold Ashton the Way makes its final crossing of the A46 and leads along Greenway Lane, which offers as tranquil and pastoral a scene as you could wish. You then walk through that pastoral landscape and up onto a hilltop called The Battlefields where there stands a monument to Sir Bevil Granville, who was killed in the Battle of Lansdown during the Civil War in 1643. From here the route goes to the scarp edge at Hanging Hill, across a golf course and along the edge of Bath Racecourse to Prospect Stile and a stimulating view worth savouring. It's virtually all downhill from here, round the flanks of Kelston Round Hill, via Penn Hill and the suburbs of Weston to the elegant streets and gardens of historic Bath.

* * *

Continue through Cold Ashton heading west, then slope down to cross the A46 for the last time. On the opposite side, Greenway Lane takes you into a lovely landscape of gentle hills - no scarp line here, but rolling wood-crowned hills folding into a bowl of tranquility, the hillsides patterned by walls or hedgerows, a spinney here, an isolated tree there. It's soft and homely; a tender, kind-hearted landscape.

Passing one or two farm buildings the lane's fall steepens and becomes more narrow. At the foot of the hill the lane curves sharply left and you leave it to go right through a gate and among a few trees (a boggy section), then over a stile into a field. Follow the left-hand boundary hedge until it cuts away. Now maintain direction ahead across the field, pass through a gateway and over the next two fields towards a barn. Leave the field beside the barn and turn left along a narrow lane. (Grid ref: 735710).

The lane forks. Bear right over a cattle-grid on a private road leading to Goudie's Farm. In a dip there's a second cattle-grid and a stream ford. Now leave the lane and head up the right-hand hillside bearing half-right. Two steeply sloping fields linked by a stile bring you to a flattish hilltop field. Walk ahead over this to another stile which brings you onto a track. Bear right and walk along this track,

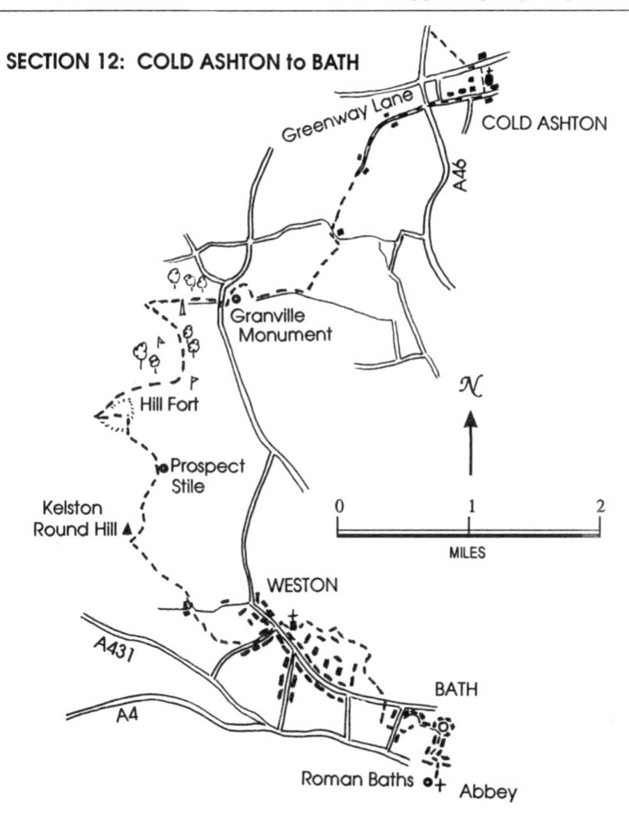

near the top of which you cross a stone stile in a wall and head along the right-hand side of a field beside the wall. When the wall ends, slant away half-right on a narrow footpath into a small woodland, alongside a low mossy wall, then over a stile to the Granville Monument (1) - a fussy memorial surrounded by iron railings (Grid ref: 722704).

Passing this on your right, walk across the meadow to exit onto a road (The Jurassic Way), cross half-right to a narrow access road leading to the United Kingdom Warning and Monitoring Organisation Sector Control.

The road forks and you take the right branch, then head left on a footpath that follows the Sector Control perimeter fence. Go through a gate and straight ahead along the top edge of a sloping meadow. (Once more the Way has returned to the scarp edge to regain broad views of sweeping hills and lowlands picked out with farms and villages.) At the western end of the promontory (Hanging Hill), cross a stile on your left, beyond which is a trig point, and walk along the scarp edge heading south-east. The views again are magnificent.

The path leads to a golf course where you hug the right-hand wall, and in a few yards drop to a stony drive and bear left. Follow the drive/track as it curves to the right with a woodland on your left. When you come to the end of the wood, head to the right on another track to pass a low building where you come to a crossing track. Bear left, then right to walk along the right-hand edge of the continuing golf course with a woodland on your right.

Leave the golf course by way of a metal gate and go straight ahead on the continuing track, sloping gently down towards that graceful panorama. About 100 yards beyond the gate leave the track to rise half-left towards a field gate. Cross over the stile beside it, then into what is at first a fairly narrow meadow but begins to open out. You stay high as you wind leftwards (heading east) onto the ramparts of Little Down Hill Fort (2) which you've been crossing. This is the last of many such Iron Age sites visited since leaving Chipping Campden.

Head to the right along the grassy rampart. On reaching a wall bear left along the scarp edge again, with views through the trees down to the River Avon. The Way brings you to Bath Racecourse. Continue along the scarp towards a stile (Prospect Stile on the map) with views growing towards the great bowl of countryside where Bath nestles gleaming (hopefully) in the sunlight. The hills seem to gather in an amphitheatre behind the city as if to hold it in an embrace. A delightful view, but at Prospect Stile is one of the loveliest views of the whole walk - not just of Bath, but of Kelston Round Hill to the south with its crown of trees. Beyond that, and to the west, there's a huge expanse of low-lying land. You gaze down to meadows and trees 600 feet below and out to a watery dazzle of light. This is a place in which to linger, Prospect Stile is a view to savour. (Grid ref: 713683). There is a topograph, provided by the Cotswold Voluntary Warden Service in 1990.

Cross the stile and head off to the left, sloping downhill among bushes. On reaching a track bear right along it, walking now towards Kelston Round Hill. The track, then footpath, leads round the left-hand (eastern) slopes of this prominent hill and onto an enclosed footpath beside a bridleway. Out of the tree-enclosure the path leads on with fine meadows on either side and more lovely views into the distance. (It's a grand way to enter a city.)

On coming to the head of a lane at Pendean Farm, take the continuing footpath which skirts the left-hand side of the farm, going along the top edge of a sloping meadow. A stile in the far corner leads onto a path which takes you down to a playing field on the edge of Weston. Cross to the far right-hand corner and come onto Anchor Road which you follow downhill *(Accommodation, refreshments, shops)*. (**Note:** the final stage of this walk is mostly along pavemented streets. There are still pleasures to be gained, but should you wish to conclude the walk here, buses run from Weston into Bath proper.)

At the bottom of Anchor Road cross over to the lower street level (High Street), then walk half-right into the raised Church Street which you follow to Weston's parish church. Walk through the churchyard to Church Road and turn left, going uphill. At the very top a tarmac path continues to a crossing road (Purlewent Drive) where you head to the right.

On coming to a close branching uphill to the left, walk up it to the top and take the footpath half-left between some houses. You then skirt the back of houses, down the right-hand edge of a meadow, (recently planted with trees) across the head of a street and into a second meadow. Another enclosed footpath now takes you steeply uphill, across a road then continue uphill again on a tarmac path - this is rather steep, but eased with steps and a handrail. You will come out at Summerhill Road, another residential street.

Leave this by bearing right into Sion Hill, then follow this road as

The Roman Baths and Bath Abbey

it curves leftwards. You come to a footpath enclosed by iron railings sloping right beside a golf course. At the bottom cross Weston Road and take the road running down the left-hand edge of the Royal Victoria Park. At the bottom take the street to the left which leads past the Victoria Monument.

Beyond the monument go to the left on a crossing road, then bear right on a tarmac path with the curving Royal Crescent seen on your left across the neatly trimmed greensward. On a crossing tarmac path go left, then turn right along Brock Street. This takes you to The Circus, a tight circle of houses which you skirt to the right and exit at the first opportunity into Gay Street. Walk down this to Queen Square, turn left into Wood Street which leads into Quiet Street. From Quiet Street bear right into Burton Street, walk straight ahead along Union Street and into elegant Stall Street, along which you turn left to see Bath Abbey facing you and the Pump Room and Roman baths on the right. It is a sight to remember, a fitting climax to a long and lovely walk. (3) *(Accommodation, refreshments, shops, post office, British Rail etc.).*

Things Seen on the Way:

(1) **The Granville Monument** marks an area known as The Battlefields on Lansdown Hill where, on July 5th, 1643, Royalist troops pursued a Parliamentarian army led by Sir William Waller into what became the Battle of Lansdown. During the pursuit up the hill, Waller's men fired their cannon into the Royalists, but Sir Bevil Granville stormed the hill on horseback in an attempt to stop the guns. He was successful but, at the moment his Cornishmen broke through, he was hit and mortally wounded. He was carried to Cold Ashton Manor where he died the same night. (Of some 2,000 Royalists taking part in the battle, only 600 are thought to have survived it.) The monument was erected in 1720 by Sir Bevil's grandson, Lord Lansdown.

(2) **Little Down Hill Fort** is the most westerly point on the Cotswold Way, an Iron Age site of about 15 acres with a rampart and single ditch still easily identified.

(3) **Bath** was known to the Romans as *Aquae Sulis* - the waters of the sun - and it was these waters that brought the city its fame. They rise at a constant temperature of 50°C (120°F), gushing at a rate of around 250,000 gallons per day. The Romans were here for 400 years, but after them the Saxons found the place "a ghostly ruin." They rebuilt the town, founded an abbey and in 973 AD Dunstan, Archbishop of Canterbury, crowned the first King of all England here. The magnificent abbey seen today, resplendent with carvings and fan-vaulted ceilings, was started in the 15th century to replace an even larger Norman cathedral. The city today, of course, has more than the fame gained by exploitation of its waters. It is one of the most architecturally satisfying of any English city: the elegant showpiece symmetry of the Royal Crescent, The Circus, Queen Square and Lansdown Crescent (built of cream-coloured local stone) all come from the 18th century after Queen Anne had set the fashion and Beau Nash made Bath the social heart of the country. If the social aspect of the waters has long since vanished, Bath has perhaps gained in the overall charm of the heritage that remains. That heritage is of the Romans, the spirit that lies behind the glory of its abbey and the architectural genius of the Regency period. Also, of course, it is the geological heritage that gives Bath in particular - and the Cotswolds in general - a stone that has bequeathed to this part of Britain a unique and endearing character. *(Tourist Information Office: 8 Abbey Churchyard, Bath. Tel: Bath 62831).*

* * *

NORTH-BOUND ROUTE
BATH to CHIPPING CAMPDEN

INTRODUCTION

Walking northward along the Cotswold escarpment has certain advantages and no shortage of advocates. For one thing the prevailing weather is at the walker's back (but then so is the sun), and some of the finest views are to be seen when approaching from the direction of Bath. The route becomes more rural the farther north you go, and with it a gentle introduction to the essential qualities of the region so that, in many ways, one steadily develops over the ensuing miles a deep awareness of the intrinsic nature of the Cotswolds - both countryside and habitation.

From Bath the route climbs onto Lansdown's broad-vista'd escarpment, visits the first of many Iron Age hill forts, crosses a golf course and the site of a decisive Civil War battle, then goes through a lovely bowl of folding hills to reach Cold Ashton. Between Cold Ashton and Tormarton there's a knot of major roads, but these are soon left behind and traded for the peace of Dodington Park where Capability Brown's handiwork becomes the very tapestry of the walker's landscape. Old Sodbury leads by way of another great Iron Age site to Little Sodbury, and from here to Horton on an easy course of low-lying fields. However, near historic Horton Court the Way takes you up to a high plateau with hinted views through the trees and a long green track to Hawkesbury Upton.

Passing the tall monument tower built in memory of one of Wellington's generals, the route now drops into a soft valley to be accompanied for a while by a clear millstream. Alderley is the first 'real' Cotswold village to be discovered on a day which ends in the one time wool town of Wotton-under-Edge. A steep climb out of town takes you back onto the wolds, emerging from woodlands to be confronted by another lofty monument, this one on Nibley Knoll in honour of William Tyndale who translated the Bible into English during the 16th century.

Just before reaching Dursley the Cotswold Way makes a tour of Stinchcombe Hill where huge panoramas are a tease of what is to come further north. Then out of Dursley another steep climb leads over a pair of outliers, Cam Peak and Cam Long Down, onto the scarp again with opportunities to visit the Uleybury hill fort and Hetty Pegler's Tump, past yet another ancient site and into woodlands before dropping to Middle Yard near the industrial belt spilling out from Stroud.

The 9½ mile stage from Middle Yard to Painswick is utterly delightful; huge views over the Severn and the Vale of Gloucester draw the eye in pleasure, and you then drop down into a green valley lit by the white-stoned charm of a small town with fine buildings and a memorable churchyard. On then to Birdlip, through more charming countryside with viewpoints to dream on, and beyond Birdlip by way of more historic sites and photogenic vistas to the literal high point of the walk on Cleeve Common above Cheltenham.

By now the character of the Cotswolds has become well established, but in many ways the best is yet to come. The route to Winchcombe shows the finest Neolithic long barrow actually on the Way (Belas Knap), passes the site of a Roman villa and magnificent Sudeley Castle, then enters an historic little town whose many houses along the main street show what grace of form can be achieved with the use of local stone.

More history waits to be unravelled between Winchcombe and Stanton, while Stanton itself is one of the unrivalled gems of the whole walk - a village of near perfection set in a warm, honey-coloured stone. From it a final 10 mile stage takes in such viewpoints as that from Broadway Tower and Dover's Hill, a brief exploration of the overly popular village of Broadway, and a wonderful finalé through the streets of elegant Chipping Campden to complete 102 miles of splendour.

* * *

For additional information on sites and scenes of particular interest, please consult the notes given at the end of parallel sections described earlier in the South-bound Route. Reference numbers quoted here in the text (running in reverse order by virtue of direction of travel) refer to specific paragraphs of explanation given in the first part of the route guide.

Morris Dancers in Bath

SECTION 1: BATH TO COLD ASHTON

(See Map page 107)

Distance:	10 miles.
Map:	O.S. Landranger series; Sheet 172 (Bristol, Bath & Surrounding Area), 1:50,000.
Accommodation:	Bath - hotels, guest-houses, b&b, youth hostel. Weston - guest-house. Nimlett - b&b, camping (three-quarters of a mile off-route). Cold Ashton - b&b.

From the glorious abbey in the heart of Roman Bath to a small village gazing south onto a quiet agricultural landscape, this first stage of the walk offers a variety of scenic pleasures. There are broad panoramas, secretive dales and sites of historic interest to set you in your stride, and once the built-up areas of Bath and Weston have been left behind, waymarking is very good and remains so (with one or two minor exceptions) not only as far as Cold Ashton, but on every part of the walk to Chipping Campden.

The architectural delights of Regency Bath lead to workaday Weston, and from there on a long, and at times, steepish haul to the lip of the escarpment where, if you pause to gaze back, a wonderful view rewards the efforts of gaining it. Over an Iron Age hill fort, round the perimeter of a golf course and along the scarp edge as the Way leads on to the Granville Monument in an area known as The Battlefields, the site of the Civil War's 1643 Battle of Lansdown. Then it's down into a bowl of meadows and fields, followed by hedge-lined Greenway Lane which takes you up the other side, eventually to reach Cold Ashton glowing in its lovely southerly aspect. This final part of the walk, from The Battlefields to Cold Ashton, virtually follows the route taken by Sir Bevil Granville's men when they brought their mortally wounded leader from the hilltop blood-bath to Cold Ashton Manor where he died.

There are no opportunities for refreshment between Weston and Cold Ashton, so take food and drink with you

The walk begins at the west front of the abbey (which is conveniently reached from Bath Spa Railway Station). With your back to the abbey and the Roman baths and Pump Room to the left, walk a few paces to find Stall Street and then Burton Street. Turn left to go from Burton Street to Quiet Street, then straight ahead into Wood Street. This leads directly to Queen Square. Head to the right now and walk up Gay Street, which will take you into The Circus, a classic amphitheatre of tightly packed houses all of a style and built around 1754.

Bear left round The Circus and leave it by way of Brock Street. On coming to Royal Crescent go across a neatly manicured greensward onto Royal Avenue and continue ahead to pass the Victoria Monument. Now bear right on a road which takes you alongside the Royal Victoria Park, cross Weston Road and follow the footpath opposite as it climbs alongside a golf course. You emerge from this into a street called Sion Hill where you turn left and walk along to Summerhill Road. Go left again and, at the end of Summerhill Road, find a descending alleyway-cum-path the steepness of which is eased by steps and a handrail.

On coming to a road, cross over and continue down another steep enclosed footpath to a kissing gate, through a brief meadow and another beyond it (now with the backs of houses to your left). A passageway takes you into a residential street where you walk down into Purlewent Drive and turn right. Soon after Lucklands Road you will find an enclosed tarmac footpath on the left which leads directly into Church Road. Go through the churchyard on the right and emerge into Church Street, Weston (Grid ref: 730664) *(Accommodation, refreshments, shops).*

Leave Church Street by going half-left to the High Street, over a traffic island and into Anchor Road. Walk uphill until you come to a large playing field on the right. Enter the playing field and cross it, walking more or less parallel with the road, to find a stile leading out the other side. Climb the grass slope ahead then, over a stile, bear right to locate the trig point on Penn Hill, the first countryside hill of the walk.

Continue ahead and follow the right-hand hedge to another stile.

Cross over and walk along the top edge of a sloping meadow to come onto a lane by Pendean Farm. The lane becomes a bridleway track with a separate footpath beside it, goes over Dean Hill and makes a curve round the eastern slopes of Kelston Round Hill - a lovely summit crowned with trees, soon to be seen to full advantage from Prospect Stile.

North of Kelston Round Hill the route goes alongside a field and begins to rise on bush-pocked slopes. A waymark post directs you left up a climbing footpath to reach Prospect Stile (Grid ref: 713683) where you should pause to contemplate the magnificent view behind you.

Bear left and follow the edge of the escarpment to a stile by the start of Bath Racecourse. Over this continue ahead and, on coming to the ditch and rampart of Little Down Hill Fort (2), turn right and soon after go to the left to wander through the central part of the fort. Over a stile bear half-right and find a track leading to a metal gate on the right. Go through the gate and wander along the track beside a golf course with Pipley Wood on your left.

Continue on the edge of the golf course, over a crosstrack to pass a low building on your right (where the wood curves off leftwards), and come to another junction of tracks. Turn left and walk ahead, now with a woodland to your right. Eventually the track veers left and descends towards a gate. Now head to the right, pass through a gap in a wall and shortly after leave the golf course to follow the left-hand wall along the edge of the escarpment again, with more fine views to enjoy.

You will come to a trig point on the promontory of Hanging Hill. Now go over a stile, turn right and walk on to find a gate which gives access onto an enclosed path which leads alongside the perimeter fence of the United Kingdom Warning and Monitoring Organisation Sector Control. On coming to an access road continue ahead to Lansdown Road. Turn right, and a short distance along this you will find a stile on the left giving into a meadow where you cut back and, at the far end, come to the rather fussy Granville Monument (1) (Grid ref: 722704).

Beyond the monument find a stile in a low mossy wall on the right, cross it and follow the wall and fence leading round to the left. Walling continues and you come to another stone stile over which you find a track. Bear left and walk along this, steadily descending from Lansdown Hill.

When you come to a gateway on the track bear left to cross a stile into a flattish hilltop field. Across this a second stile brings you to another field and, maintaining direction, you descend this and another steeply sloping field to come to the farm access road leading to Goudie's Farm. Go left, over a stream, a cattle-grid and a second grid beyond that. Continue ahead towards a barn, then head to the right to cross three fields. At the far side of the third of these look for a stile which will take you into a spinney that is rather boggy underfoot. Out of this you come onto Greenway Lane where you head to the left and walk uphill, passing one or two farm buildings.

As you stroll up the lane allow your eyes to wander across the bowl of countryside falling behind and to the side of you. It's a lovely gentle landscape, especially when seen on a bright sunny afternoon, with cows in the pastures and birds and rabbits among the hedgerows.

Greenway Lane brings you to the busy A46 - a road that will be crossed and recrossed a number of times in the days ahead. On this occasion you cross to the eastern side and walk uphill on a continuing road which leads into the village of Cold Ashton (Grid ref: 751727) *(Accommodation, refreshments).*

For information about Cold Ashton, see details at the end of Section 11 of the South-bound Route.

* * *

SECTION 2: COLD ASHTON TO TORMARTON

(See Map page 102)

Distance:	6 miles.
Map:	O.S. Landranger series; Sheet 172 (Bristol, Bath & Surrounding Area), 1:50,000.
Accommodation:	Tormarton - b&b.

With only 6 miles to cover this stage could be walked in a morning, but for those with time to spare, a lengthy distraction in the National Trust's Dyrham Park would be worth considering. Elsewhere there's agricultural land and a couple of woods to wander through, finishing with a mile or so of road walking. Tormarton at the end of the stage is also an interesting place in its own right. Refreshments are available here, as well as in the hamlet of Pennsylvania only a mile after setting out.

From Cold Ashton the route goes across fields to the A46 at Pennsylvania, and from there by way of woods and more fields to the edge of Dyrham village. The route does not actually pass through Dyrham Park, and if this is on your itinerary you'll have to make a diversion of a mile to the official entrance. Unless, that is, you're a member of the National Trust, in which case it is permissible to enter via the churchyard.

The Way passes round the outside of the perimeter wall with fine views to enjoy and as clear an indication of long past cultivation in the form of strip lynchets as you're likely to see anywhere in the Cotswolds. Over Hinton Hill you pass an historic site where, in 577 AD, the ancient Britons fought the Saxons and lost, thereby giving the Saxons control of Gloucester, Cirencester and Bath. Finally a series of fields brings you to more woods through which you emerge to a mile of road walking into Tormarton.

* * *

Wander through Cold Ashton, with the manor and old rectory side by side on the left and lovely views off to the right, then bear left into the churchyard and out the other side. Continue ahead to reach the

A420 opposite The White Hart. Cross to the pub and head left alongside the road until you come to a field on the right with a gate leading into it. Go across the field aiming half-left, cross a stile and maintain direction over the next field to its far corner where another stile gives access to the busy A46 on the edge of the hamlet of Pennsylvania (Grid ref: 744733) *(Refreshments)*.

Go over the road and along the bridleway opposite. This brings you to a minor road that is, nonetheless, often busy with traffic. Turn left and walk along this road for about 80 yards, then enter a gate on the right leading into a hilltop meadow. Walk across this towards a barn and a woodland beyond. A stile takes you into Dyrham Wood and, ignoring paths to left and right, continue directly ahead and sloping downhill to emerge on the far side into a large field. Bear right to a woodland shaw where you will find a gate and plank footbridge over a stream.

Now cross a hilly field veering a little to the left to join a hedgerow coming from the right. Maintain direction and follow the hedgerow to a gap, go through it and across the centre of the next field and head down to a pond. Continue ahead, following hedgerows through a series of fields linked by more stiles, and come at last to a minor road leading into Dyrham village. Turn left on the road, and when you come to a junction shortly after, bear right to pass the gateway of Dyrham House and Park on your right (1).

With the entrance to the church on the right, the road swings left to pass some lovely mellow cottages. Opposite these you head off to the right and along a short, sunken track to follow the boundary wall of Dyrham Park. As you wander alongside the wall views open out, and before long you will notice a series of strip lynchets (noted as 'field system' on the O.S. map). Beyond these a clump of trees marks the site of a hill fort where the Saxons and Britons met in battle in 577 AD (2).

The wall eventually brings you to a country road (Field Lane) where you turn left. On coming to a T-junction cross ahead, pass through a gate and maintain direction along the left-hand edge of fields, passing beneath power lines and coming to another gate. Go through this and turn right to follow the right-hand field boundary, soon with woodlands on your right. At the end of the field bear left and continue along its boundary until directed by waymarks into the wood and out the other side to a car park and picnic area *(public toilets)*. Continue ahead on a tarmac footpath leading to the A46.

Cross the road with great care, bear left and walk ahead, over the M4 motorway and then along the A46 which you leave at the first road on the right. At the next junction go right again. After nearly half a mile you will find a footpath sign directing you left to Tormarton. Over a stone stile the path goes round two sides of a field to another stone stile. Cross this and the field beyond to come into Tormarton by The Portcullis Inn (Grid ref: 767786) *(Accommodation, refreshments)*.

For information about Tormarton see details at the end of Section 10 of the South-bound Route.

* * *

SECTION 3: TORMARTON TO HAWKESBURY UPTON

(See Map page 95)

Distance:	8 miles.
Map:	O.S. Landranger series; Sheet 172 (Bristol, Bath & Surrounding Area), 1:50,000
Accommodation:	Old Sodbury - hotel, b&b. Horton - b&b (three-quarters of a mile off-route). Hawkesbury Upton - b&b.

After the residential streets of Bath and Weston that began the Cotswold Way, followed by the interruption of major roads on Section 2, this part of the walk has a distinctly rural quality about it. There are three or four small villages on the route, and here and there some quiet lanes to wander. But it is the countryside aspect that dominates; the great parkland laid out by Capability Brown, the fields and meadows, the glancing long views, the breezy upland spaces where stone barns hunch their eaves and old trees spread their uppermost branches in expressions of wild gesticulation. There's a large Iron Age hill fort to traverse, and nearby a tiny hamlet where William Tyndale preached more than four centuries ago. It's a peaceful land. Not yet the essential Cotswolds, perhaps, but one senses the drawing power of the wolds; a hint of good things to come.

Almost as soon as Tormarton has been left behind, the Way plunges into Dodington Park where you walk in the shadow of lovely specimen trees and practically trip over pheasant and guinea fowl. Out then to Coombes End where field paths make a detour to Old Sodbury. This is soon traded for Little Sodbury, followed by more fields that lead to Horton. Horton Court is an historic place dating from 1140. Owned today by the National Trust, it's worth a visit if you have the time.

Up then, onto a rough plateau where the Way joins a former trading route called Bath Lane. This is a track, a green lane that holds plenty of water in a rainy season, and it takes you directly to Hawkesbury Upton.

Refreshments are available on this stage in Old Sodbury.

* * *

There are easy, straightforward road routes out of Tormarton, but the Cotswold Way ignores them and chooses instead to make a tour of the village. Passing The Portcullis Inn on your right turn left on the road towards the church, then go left again over a stile into a meadow. Walk ahead across this to a barn and leave the meadow by way of another stile onto a village street. Bear left, then cross into a field on the right beside The Old School House. Now walk ahead across the field, over a narrow road and another field to a second narrow road. A final field crossing is made, on the far side of which you come to a stone stile leading out to the A46 by an old milestone.

With due caution cross the road to its western side and drop down to a gate leading into a field. Go down this field to a footbridge leading over a stream, which is the infant River Frome, cross a stile and head half-left (north-west) over the next field and make for the left-hand edge of a woodland. Continue in the same direction and, when the wood finishes, cross a stile by a field gate and descend the slope half-right (crossing other stiles on the way) until you come to the drive leading to Dodington House (4) (unseen off to the left). Cross the drive and walk ahead through a field to reach a quiet road at Coombes End (Grid ref: 753805).

Bear right and walk along the road rising uphill. You will pass a turning to the left. Ignore this and continue to a cottage beyond which you'll see a gate on the left. In the field follow a hedge on your right (northwards), pass through a gap and down the slope to a stile. Climb over this and head across the field aiming half-left towards the far corner, passing a small pond as you go. Leave the field through a gate and turn right along Chapel Lane.

About 400 yards later you come to the A432 by the side of The Dog Inn at Old Sodbury (Grid ref: 754816) *(Accommodation, refreshments, shop).* Cross the road into a farmyard and to the right of a black barn find a stile leading into a field. Half-right across this another stile in the corner takes you into a sloping meadow. Walk up this towards the church, go through a kissing gate and wander through the churchyard to the lych gate. The village school stands nearby. Take the enclosed footpath next to it which leads past Hayes Farm and into a field. Continue ahead along the lower boundary of the field to cross a stile eventually and come onto a path which climbs the slope to the right among trees.

At the head of the slope go through a gate on the left and enter the earth ramparts of Sodbury Hill Fort (3). Head north across the shallow centre of the earthworks and out the other side, just before some farm buildings. Bear left, cross a stile by the buildings, then go right to meet a farm track and head to the left down it to come to a country road.

On the road turn right and walk along it to a junction by Little Sodbury's church, which is dedicated to St Adeline (2) (Grid ref: 757833). Turn right, a few paces later go left beside a cottage, then walk half-right by the back door into a field. Follow the left-hand boundary hedge and maintain direction through successive fields, passing below a farm reservoir in a dip and up the other side, still in the same direction, then through the middle of a last field, over a stile and out to the village street in Horton.

Turn right, and a few paces later, at a junction, head off to the left by the village school on a lane that leads to Horton Court (1). Along this lane some lovely wide views are to be had. On a bend in the lane just before Horton Court and church, bear right through a gate and climb the sloping meadow, then pass through another gate and into a beechwood. The Way continues uphill, but you soon break away to the left, up a few steps and out of the trees by way of a stile into a scrubby meadow.

After a few paces a waymark directs you half-right ahead, then alongside a field, through a gap in some bushes, across towards a stone barn and beyond it to a stile. Now walk ahead, keeping to the right-hand boundary of two fields and parallel with Highfield Lane. Towards the end of the second field swing left round a shed and come to a track known as Bath Lane where it joins Highfield Lane. Bear left and walk along Bath Lane for about a mile. (This one-time trading route can be very wet at times.)

Bath Lane eventually brings you out onto a minor road on the northern edge of Hawkesbury Upton. Bear right and you will shortly come to a triangle of roads containing a duck pond (Grid ref: 775874) *(Accommodation, refreshments, shop, post office).*

For information about Hawkesbury Upton, see details at the end of Section 9 of the South-bound Route.

* * *

SECTION 4: HAWKESBURY UPTON TO WOTTON-UNDER-EDGE

(See Map page 90)

Distance:	8 miles.
Map:	O.S. Landranger series; Sheet 172 (Bristol, Bath & Surrounding Area), 1:50,000.
Accommodation:	Hillesley - b&b (three-quarters of a mile off-route). Wortley - b&b (half a mile off-route). Wotton-under-Edge - b&b (camping three-quarters of a mile off-route).

North of Hawkesbury Upton the escarpment sends wooded finger spurs out to the west. Between them streams come bubbling; millstreams, clean and cheerful companions for valley walks. There are still a few mills left standing beside these streams, and on the gentle stroll through the Kilcott Valley we pass one of them.

There are woodlands, too, a deeply sunken track cut by centuries of use and a welcome return to the scarp edge with its big panoramas (the onward route beckoning as you gaze towards tomorrow). And there's Alderley; a small hamlet snug in its warm Cotswold stone midway between two green valleys. This is a walk of considerable charm, best taken at an easy, unhurried pace.

It begins by passing below the lofty Somerset Monument, erected in 1846 in memory of General Somerset of nearby Badminton, who served under Wellington at the Battle of Waterloo. It then takes to fields and woods before slipping into the Kilcott Valley whose stream is followed north-westward for a while. Passing out of Avon and into Gloucestershire the Way now approaches Alderley, then crosses fields to the edge of Wortley before climbing onto the escarpment at Tor Hill. Bridleways, footpaths and a narrow lane take the route from Tor Hill into a final valley for another millstream walk into Wotton-under-Edge.

There are no refreshments available on this walk.

At the duck pond in Hawkesbury Upton turn left along the road, soon to pass the Somerset Monument (3). (For a small fee it is possible to climb the 144 steps to a viewing platform.) Keep on the road, ignoring the turn-off to the left, but just beyond a dutch barn leave the road through a field gate on the right. Walk straight ahead, soon along the right-hand side of a dividing hedge, then on to the far left-hand corner of the field to enter Frith Wood by a gate. Maintain direction to Frith Wood which you enter by a gate. The route leads along the right-hand edge of the wood at first, then joins a bridleway going deeper into it.

Leave the wood at a stile next to a field gate and continue ahead, passing along the left-hand side of a hedgerow to a sunken bridleway track going downhill among trees. You emerge in the Kilcott Valley opposite some cottages in the hamlet of Lower Kilcott (Grid ref: 787890).

Turn left and walk along the country lane with the Kilcott Brook for company for about three-quarters of a mile, passing as you do Kilcott Mill with its attractive stone buildings and mill pond on your right. Soon after passing the mill a track breaks away to the right into the Tresham valley. (**Note**: if refreshments or accommodation are required at this stage, ignore this track and continue along the lane for a further three-quarters of a mile to Hillesley.)

The route turns along the track for about 200 yards, then you head to the left on an enclosed track-cum-path to a metal gate. Continue ahead in the same direction along the left-hand edge of several fields linked by stiles or gates, then along a gently rising farm track into Alderley near the village church (2). Turn right and walk along the road (signposted to Tresham) to a junction and go straight across into a narrow, metalled lane. After a few yards the lane curves right and a path continues ahead. It bears left at the bottom of a slope. Cross the stream coming from Ozleworth Bottom and climb over a stile by a field gate into a small field. Another stile on the far side of this takes you into a larger field where the route is directed by a large sign on an electricity pole. The way goes diagonally across this field towards the far right-hand corner where you come to a lane on the outskirts of Wortley (1) *(Accommodation).*

Cross the lane and walk along the farm track opposite. On the edge of a woodland bear right and walk up the sunken track (a magical section of ivy-clung banks and lush fronds of hart's tongue fern) leading onto the escarpment. Once out of the trees continue ahead and keep along the left-hand boundary of the fields. Look for the waymark which sends you off to the left through a narrow strip of woodland and out onto a terrace of meadowland on the very scarp edge. (Fine views from here.)

Walk across the terrace to the far side and once through a field gate bear right to follow a fence, then a wall, heading east. You eventually come to a narrow road where you head sharp left, now walking a little north of west along Blackquarries Hill. After a little over half a mile, leave the road on a bridleway heading down to the right among trees. This brings you to another country road by The Hive. Turn right and walk into Coombe until you come to a stream where you bear left and walk alongside it to Wotton-under-Edge.

The footpath leads into Valley Road and this, in turn, takes you to Coombe Road. Bear left and shortly after you will reach the Church of St Mary the Virgin. The continuing route leads through the churchyard (Grid ref: 760935) *(Accommodation, refreshments, shops, post office etc.).*

For information about Wotton-under-Edge, see details at the end of Section 8 of the South-bound Route.

* * *

Kelston Round Hill from Prospect Stile (Section 12)

Above: First view of Bath from Prospect Stile (Section 12)

Below: The Royal Bath Crescent, Bath

SECTION 5: WOTTON-UNDER-EDGE TO DURSLEY

(See Map page 83)

Distance:	7 miles.
Map:	O.S. Landranger series; Sheet 162 (Gloucester & Forest of Dean Area), 1:50,000.
Accommodation:	North Nibley - b&b, camping. Dursley - hotel.

Another short stage this may be, but there are two major climbs to be made; the first soon after setting out (leading onto Wotton Hill) and the second on the approach to Dursley (the ascent of Stinchcombe Hill). Both heights give splendid views, as does Nibley Knoll to the north-west of Wotton where a memorial tower stands as a reminder of the life and work of William Tyndale. History is on these heights, and also down below between North Nibley and Nibley Green.

The route passes through Wotton-under-Edge with the opportunity to study some interesting and attractive buildings, then begins the sharp climb onto Wotton Hill with its plantation of trees and lovely viewpoint. Next into woods and alongside another Iron Age hill fort, then out to a meadowland on Nibley Knoll before dropping to the village of North Nibley where the last battle took place in England between private retainer armies. A track and two or three field paths make an open approach to Stinchcombe Hill. Last comes the ascent of the scarp slope, followed by a tour round the upper plateau and a descent among woods on the eastern side to the busy little town of Dursley.

Refreshments are available in North Nibley.

* * *

Going through the churchyard of St Mary the Virgin, pass the church on your left, walk down an alleyway, then bear right into a second alleyway called The Cloud. Out of this cross to Church Street and walk along it to the end, bearing right then into Long Street with shops on either side. Long Street becomes High Street, at the end of which is a minor crossroads. Go straight ahead into Bradley Street. This leads directly to the B4060 (Grid ref: 753936).

Bear left and soon you will notice the junction with Old London Road. Just beyond this cross the road and take the steep path climbing on the right. There are handrails to assist. This path brings you to a narrow lane, across which a set of steps and a stile take you to the foot of a steep meadow. Climb this meadowland slope to the Jubilee Plantation - a clump of commemorative trees contained within a circular wall (5).

Continue to the top left-hand corner of the meadow where a stile leads into a large field beside a woodland. Maintain direction along the left-hand field boundary and on a track leading into Westridge Wood. The track forks and meets several alternative paths, but waymarks aid direction-finding. On the way through the wood you pass along the right-hand edge of the somewhat overgrown hill fort site of Brackenbury Ditches. (4).

On emerging from the woods, follow the left-hand fence of the open meadowland of Nibley Knoll and walk towards the towering Tyndale Monument (3). From the base of this rather solemn looking tower magnificent views are to be enjoyed on a clear day. A topograph nearby highlights noteworthy places to be seen. (It is possible to climb the tower, but the key must first be obtained from a house in North Nibley below. The key's location is given on a notice-board at the foot of the track which leads down to the village.)

From the tower head to the right along the opposite side of the meadow to find a set of bars (in lieu of a stile) leading onto a path which goes through trees and scrub to a sunken track descending to the B4060 in the village of North Nibley (2) *(Accommodation, refreshments, shop)*. (Grid ref: 741957). Cross the road and bear right. A few yards later you come to a junction where you bear left into The Street. Walk along this for a short distance, then turn right by some houses into Lower House Lane.

An enclosed path continues from the lane and becomes almost a tunnel for a while. Along this section of the walk note an old doorway dated 1607 in the left-hand wall. The path comes to some trees and emerges onto the B4060 again, which you cross straight ahead to walk down a metalled lane. Soon after crossing a stream you come to some cottages and climb out of the lane over a stile on the left. Go up the sloping meadow to a second stile, then half-left through the next field to a narrow road opposite the entrance to Park Farm House (Grid ref: 744972).

Another stile is found to the left of the gateway to the house. Cross this into a hillside meadow, walk up to a fence and bear left alongside it to a stile with a waymark directing the onward route. (The path is not always evident here.) Over a stile continue to yet another stile, go down through a hollow and then up among woods on the scarp face to emerge on the golf course on Stinchcombe Hill (1).

Waymarks lead the Way on a circuitous route anti-clockwise round the golf course and the hilltop promontory, with magnificent views over a vast area. First you curve left round the head of Hollow Combe to Drakestone Point, then head north to the Tubbs shelter, and through trees. Eventually bear right across fairways to a narrow lane. At a junction go left to the golf club-house. Beside this a path breaks away to the right and descends through woodland to Dursley. You will come to Hill Road which leads in turn to May Lane. Coming to a shopping precinct on the right, walk through it as far as the Market House (1738) opposite the 15th century Parish Church of St James in the very heart of Dursley (Grid ref: 757981) *(Accommodation, refreshments, shops, post office etc.).*

For information about Dursley, see details at the end of Section 7 of the South-bound Route.

* * *

SECTION 6: DURSLEY TO MIDDLE YARD (KING'S STANLEY)

(See Map page 76)

Distance:	$6^1/2$ miles.
Map:	O.S. Landranger series; Sheet 162 (Gloucester & Forest of Dean Area), 1:50,000.
Accommodation:	Nympsfield - b&b, camping (half a mile off-route). Middle Yard - b&b

The modest distance covered by this section belies the energetic nature of the route. There is much height to be gained and lost; the crossing of two classic outliers (Cam Peak and Cam Long Down) and the ascent and re-ascent of the steep scarp face. There are interesting archaeological sites, both on the route and a short distance from it, woodland walks and yet more extensive views to enjoy.

Out of Dursley one is at first lulled into a sense of ease, then suddenly there comes the very steep climb up Cam Peak (Peaked Down on the O.S. map), a hard pull on cropped grass with a superb view from the top. Then down to a saddle before climbing again, this time onto the higher summit of Cam Long Down. A steep descent follows, then wandering along a lane to the foot of the main scarp face. A sunken track takes you almost to the top near the earthworks of Uleybury promontory fort, then a short traverse is made before dropping through trees to the foot of the slope once more. Having reached the low point, you then have to re-ascend once more to Frocester Hill, pass the Nympsfield long barrow and plunge among woods on a long up and down traverse of the scarp before heading down to Middle Yard to the south-west of Stroud.

This is a fine walk, constantly interesting, varied and scenic. However, note that there are no opportunities for refreshment after leaving Dursley, and none at all in Middle Yard. The moral is clear - pack food and drink to take with you.

* * *

From the Market House in Dursley bear left and walk down Long Street, leaving it when the road makes a sharp left turn. Continue ahead and pass a bowling green on the left, go up some steps beside a red-brick house, over a stile and into a small field. A stile takes you into the next field near some farm buildings and you walk ahead along a field boundary until waymarks direct you onto a narrow country road. This is Drake Lane. Bear right along Drake Lane to a road junction, over another stile in the opposite hedge and across the field to a stile giving onto a road near Down House Farm (Grid ref: 765992). Bear right for a few yards, go through a gate and across a corner of trees and bushes, then steeply up the grass slopes of Cam Peak ahead.

Views from the summit are impressive, but they are even more so from the top of the next hill along. Go down on a grassy path between swathes of bracken to an obvious saddle, then up the next slope to the top of Cam Long Down (4), a flat-topped hill with a wonderful panorama.

Cross the summit ridge to its eastern end, then descend to scrub and trees hiding a stile. Over this continue down the hillside meadow and across a field towards some barns. Now walk ahead along a narrow country lane and when it curves to the right, break away left and follow the farm track leading to Springfield and Hodgecomb farms. The track goes between the farms to enter Coaley Wood, which it then climbs as a steep, sunken way (often rather muddy and cut by horses' hooves). It emerges almost at the top of the scarp slope near Uleybury hill fort (3). (**Note:** to visit Uleybury simply go up a little further onto the lip of the escarpment. An interesting circuit can then be made of the ramparts of this ancient site.)

To continue the Cotswold Way go over a crossing track and take the opposite path bearing left in a traverse of the hillside below an exposed quarry cliff. This then starts to descend, going down a long series of steps and reaching the foot of the slope at the head of a narrow lane (Grid ref: 790003). Ignore the lane and re-ascend the scarp slope on a sunken track, coming out by the side of the B4066 a short distance from Hetty Pegler's Tump, a Neolithic burial chamber

(2). (**Note:** if you wish to visit Hetty Pegler's Tump - or Uley Tumulus, as it is also known - turn right and walk along the road for about half a mile. A key is available at Crawley Barns to enable visitors to enter the main chamber.)

Bear left alongside the wood, then left again onto the road descending Frocester Hill. A few yards along this turn right on a woodland path, go down some steps and past a quarried cliff. Continue along the path which eventually rises onto a green hilltop meadow at Frocester Hill, with yet more splendid views. Bear left along the scarp edge to Nympsfield Long Barrow (1) and continue ahead through Coaley Peak Country Park (Grid ref: 794015) *(public toilets).*

Walk ahead to a stile beyond the car park and into woodlands again. The path takes you alongside a small fenced quarry, leading near the road. You then bear left on an obvious path, down some steps, over a crossing track and through a wooden squeeze stile. Continue downhill to emerge from the woods and walk along the upper edge of a meadow, now with the woods on your right. Pass above Woodside Farm, cut across the slope a little to find a stile leading into some jungly undergrowth and then walk through a rough area of coppice, finally rising now into Stanley Woods.

These are lovely mature beechwoods and the path makes a clear traverse through them below Pen Hill. The Way then goes down on an enclosed path, out of the woods onto Pen Lane which you descend to a squeeze stile leading into a pasture. Cross this to another stile, walk down an enclosed footpath onto a drive which takes you out to a road among houses in Middle Yard. Cross the road and bear left, in a few yards you will come to King's Stanley Baptist Church (Grid ref: 820032) *(Accommodation; refreshments half a mile NW).*

* * *

SECTION 7: MIDDLE YARD TO PAINSWICK

(See Map page 69)

Distance:	9 1/2 miles.
Map:	O.S. Landranger series; Sheet 162 (Gloucester & Forest of Dean Area), 1:50,000.
Accommodation:	King's Stanley - camping. Randwick - b&b (half a mile off-route). Painswick - hotel, b&b, camping.

This is one of the loveliest of walks on the Cotswold Way. It climbs out of Stroud's industrial valley and onto the escarpment, through woods, out to jutting prows and memorable views over birch-speckled commons with the white stone of Painswick beckoning ahead. Painswick itself makes a happy end to the day: an old market town with interesting back streets and an utterly delightful churchyard noted far and wide for its neatly trimmed yews and table tombs.

From Middle Yard the Way leads across fields to King's Stanley Mill. There follows a short stretch of road walking, but then you break away and climb a hillside on the western edge of Stroud's probing tentacles, up to high, bird-raucous Standish Wood and out to a pair of promontories with outstanding panoramas. Haresfield Beacon is the second of these, a glorious spot worth savouring. After this, it's back to woods again along the edge of Scottsquar Hill, over Edge Common and a series of meadows to finish in the bleached delight that is Painswick.

Once away from the thunderous traffic descending on Stroud there's barely a dull moment. It's a country walk of considerable variety with many a long mile of Nature's own peace. Refreshment is found on the last leg in the form of a pub as you come off Edge Common, a mile and a half from Painswick.

* * *

The continuing path leads down the left-hand side of King's Stanley Baptist Church, over a stile and across to a fence. In the next field go half-left to a stile in the corner, then along the left-hand boundary hedge of a third field. Another stile takes you into a larger field where you cross to a narrow farm road. Walk along the left-hand boundary of a farm, and on through a succession of meadows linked by stiles to a road nearly opposite King's Stanley Mill (3) (Grid ref: 813043).

Bear right along the road and very shortly you cross first the River Frome, then the Stroudwater Canal (2). Soon after the canal you come to a road junction. Cross the busy A419 and turn right. Go beneath a footbridge and a few yards beyond this, opposite a garden centre, bear left and walk ahead along the edge of a sports field, over a railway footbridge and into a field where you bear right alongside a hedge. Two more fields linked by stiles are crossed, then you walk alongside another boundary hedge to a stile beside a field gate in a dip. Over the stile climb the meadow beyond, passing beneath power cables as you do, and find a squeeze stile by an oak tree. The path continues in the same direction to a further stile which leads onto a narrow road.

Turn right for about 200 yards, then bear left between some houses (this is Westrip), over another stile, up a meadow and out onto a second narrow road. Turn left, then veer right to enter Three Bears Wood, a short strip of woodland which the path wanders through.

At the top of the wood a stone stile leads out. Cross to a gateway on the right and follow the left-hand stone wall. This brings you to a crossway at the head of a narrow lane which leads on the right to Randwick. Walk directly ahead, then veer leftwards on a bridleway entering Standish Wood (Grid ref: 824067).

The route through Standish Wood is almost 2 miles long with several crossing tracks and alternative paths that might confuse, had the Way not been so well waymarked. (At each junction look for the distinctive CW arrow and spot.) You will eventually rise out of the wood and into a National Trust car park. Bear left out of the car park and across an open hilltop meadow to find an interesting raised topograph with superb views out to the Vale of Gloucester and the windings of the River Severn glinting in the light.

From the topograph cut back to the right (heading north) to the far left-hand corner of the meadow where a waymark directs you left onto a broad path descending among trees. Cross a stile along the path and, a short distance beyond it, look out for a narrow path climbing the slope to the right. This brings you to road level, but without going onto the road you head sharp left on the waymarked path which leads through the earthworks of another hill fort (mostly confused by trees and scrub). The clear path winds leftwards round the promontory and goes directly to the trig point on Haresfield Beacon (1) (Grid ref: 820089).

This is one of the finest viewpoints of the Cotswold Way. A huge panorama overlooks the Vale of Gloucester, River Severn, the Forest of Dean and so much more. In spring the hawthorn bushes are afroth with blossom, the grasslands dazzling with wild flowers; in October autumn colours burnish the scene. There's a wondrous sense of space; a great place to spread yourself on the lush turf and allow the long walk to establish perspective. A picnic spot *par excellence.*

Return from the trig point spur heading north-east, with the slope falling away to your left. Cross a stile and follow the path ahead down to Ring Hill Farm. Bear left on the lane, then take the track on the right above Ring Hill Cottage. This leads without confusion through woods, past Cromwell's Stone (on a bend) and out to another quiet lane next to Cliffwell Cottage (Grid ref: 833095).

Bear right and walk along the lane, then leave it to take a bridleway forking left into Halliday Wood. This track can be rather muddy at times and, in places, heavily threatened by rampant growth on either side. The Way follows it for a little over half a mile, passing an unusual hexagonal house on the left, before coming to a narrow path climbing to the right.

This path leads onto a minor road just to the left of some abandoned quarries on Scottsquar Hill. Cross the road and find a narrow path working its way well to the left of the quarries. Beyond them waymark posts direct you south-eastwards down the slopes of Edge Common, with views ahead of Painswick backed by the dark green of woodland.

Waymarks bring you to a clearer path where you bear right, then a little later go left, descending to the Gloucester-Stroud road nearly opposite Edgemoor Inn *(Refreshments)*. Cross the road and walk down the narrow lane ahead. Just before coming to Jenkins Farm find a gap in the left-hand hedge and a few steps which take you across to a stile in a fence. Bear right over this and head downhill to a footbridge over a stream. A narrow path then takes you through a patch of woodland and out near some barns at Washbrook Farm.

Passing the barns go in front of the farm and turn right. Cross a stream and bear right alongside trees, then bear left beside a hedge, before cutting across a field. Bear left, cross a stile near a tennis court and continue across the next field. Now bear right and find an enclosed footpath at the back of some houses. This brings you to Hambutts Field (owned by the Open Spaces Society) which you cross along its right-hand edge. Climb over a last stile to Edge Road, turn right and walk downhill. You emerge in New Street, Painswick, opposite the lych gate of the splendid churchyard (Grid ref: 865097) *(Accommodation, refreshments, shops, post office, etc.)*.

For information about Painswick, which is well worth exploring, see details at the end of Section 5 of the South-bound Route.

* * *

SECTION 8: PAINSWICK TO BIRDLIP

(See Map page 62)

Distance: 7 miles.

Maps: O.S. Landranger series; Sheets 163 (Cheltenham & Cirencester Area) and 162 (Gloucester & Forest of Dean Area), 1:50,000.

Accommodation: Cranham Corner - b&b, camping.
Cooper's Hill - b&b, camping.
Birdlip - hotel, b&b.

Much of this stage of the walk goes through woodland, but there are open panoramic viewpoints too. The hill fort site of Painswick Beacon gives popular views, as does Cooper's Hill at the head of the famous cheese-rolling slope. Bucknolt and Brockworth Woods are Nature Reserves. There is the site of a Roman villa just off the route and also Prinknash Abbey just below the scarp slope.

Away from Painswick's dusty-white buildings the route soon climbs onto the Wolds once more, near a hamlet charmingly named Paradise. Painswick Beacon tops a trim golf course and the walk takes you alongside it, into Pope's Wood, and skirting the scarp edge, passes above Prinknash Abbey, goes through more woodlands and emerges to lovely views on Cooper's Hill. Down then to a string of cottages enjoying the fine views north, before plunging again among trees on the long unbroken woodland stretch to Birdlip.

Refreshments are to be had below Cooper's Hill.

* * *

The straightforward route through Painswick simply follows New Street uphill to the left as far as Gloucester Street, where it turns left. (There is an interesting alternative route, however, that adds very little distance and is worth taking. Cross New Street and go through the lych gate into the churchyard with its magnificent yews and table tombs. Pass the church to your right and exit the churchyard on the far side to find the town's iron 'spectacle' stocks. Bear left along St Mary's Street, then fork left into Friday Street. This leads to Bisley Street which takes you left up to New Street again. Cross this directly into Gloucester Street to resume the official way.)

Walk uphill along Gloucester Street, passing the one-way system which directs the B4073 down into town, until you come to a minor road branching off to the right. Walk along this, then veer leftwards on a footpath through trees, over a narrow lane and across the lower part of a golf course towards the left-hand side of a cemetery. Continue ahead with the cemetery wall on your right, so passing the little church that serves the parish of Paradise. Beyond the wall cross another open golf course fairway to a clear path heading through a strip of woodland (tree-screened views off to the right). Pass Catsbrain Quarry to reach a narrow lane climbing leftwards uphill across the golf course. A short distance along this, break away to the right on a waymarked path which takes you still across the golf course heading north-east below the crown of Painswick Beacon (4) (Grid ref: 868121). It is worth making a slight diversion onto the hill for the views.

The route across here is most pleasant, and on the far side you enter Pope's Wood and join a metalled lane. When this lane curves right you continue ahead on a clear track. It soon comes to a minor road that drops off the scarp to Upton St Leonards and Gloucester. Cross the road and continue ahead, then veer right alongside the boundary wall of Prinknash Park (3). Within a few yards you come to a junction of roads at Cranham Corner, also known as Prinknash Corner *(Accommodation)*.

Cross the A46 and walk ahead along the Birdlip road, then fork left on a path among fine beechwoods. Waymarks direct you along the correct path as there are several alternative tracks, some rather enticing. Brockworth and Buckholt Woods are linked by a short and well waymarked 'corridor' and the route continues to wind its way, now among ash, sycamore and birch, as well as the ubiquitous beech, until at last you emerge to an open grassy glade on Cooper's Hill (2) which bears a maypole at the head of the cheese-rolling slope (Grid ref: 892146). Splendid views are to be enjoyed from this point. The Malvern Hills and the Black Mountains are among the points of interest to be picked out on a clear day.

Descend leftwards through more trees on a curving path that brings you out to a collection of cottages on a narrow lane. Walk to the right along the lane, soon to pass a cottage advertising teas and snacks (The Haven Tea Garden). The lane becomes a track, and the track a woodland path delving deeply into Witcombe Wood. (Out of the woods below, to the left, there once stood a Roman villa (1), unfortunately the site is not on our route.)

Again, as with other extensive woodlands on this walk, an assortment of paths and tracks criss-cross among the trees. Again the correct Cotswold Way has been generously (though not too intrusively) waymarked. Simply make sure that the route you are following bears the distinctive arrow and spot CW symbol.

Eventually the path begins to climb out of the woods onto a road on Birdlip Hill. The continuing route crosses the road to a clear woodland track which rises to The Peak. For accommodation and/ or refreshments, however, bear right on the road and walk uphill for about 400 yards to the village of Birdlip *(Accommodation, refreshments, shop)* (Grid ref: 925144).

For information about Birdlip, see details at the end of Section 4 of the South-bound Route.

* * *

SECTION 9: BIRDLIP TO CLEEVE HILL

(See Map page 54)

Distance:	15 1/2 miles.
Map:	O.S. Landranger series; Sheet 163 (Cheltenham & Cirencester Area), 1:50,000.
Accommodation:	Cleeve Hill - hotel, youth hostel. Woodmancote - camping (1 1/4 miles off-route).

This is the longest section without a convenient accommodation break along the route of the Cotswold Way. It is a scenically delightful walk, if a little strenuous in places. There will be some road walking, but this is fortunately kept to a minimum. For much of the way the route traces the western edge of the escarpment high above Cheltenham. There are sections of woodland walking, some sections across ragged heath and others through an agricultural landscape.

The day begins by rejoining the path as it crosses the slopes of Birdlip Hill and winds on a woodland track to a viewpoint on The Peak. You then follow a series of paths along the scarp edge, over a busy road and into Crickley Hill Country Park with its fascinating archaeological site and open grasslands speckled with orchids in springtime. From here the scarp is traced to Shurdington Hill, then along a former drove road, followed by a return to the escarpment near Leckhampton Hill. Projecting from a lower terrace of the scarp is the Devil's Chimney, which has become virtually the symbol of the Cotswold Way. In truth you have to break off the path a little in order to see it close-to.

Beyond Leckhampton Hill the scarp is hugged again round Charlton Kings Common before veering 'inland' to Seven Springs. A choice of onward routes leads either to a mile of road walking, or to a longer countryside detour round Chatcombe Wood, before a return to the scarp and a descent through woods into a valley cupping Dowdeswell Reservoir. Up again, along woods and over meadows, along a lane and onto the breezy upland of Cleeve Common, (the highest part of the Cotswold Way and well above the 1,000 foot contour). Cleeve Hill village is tucked just below its north-western rim.

It's a grand walk.

Refreshments are available at The Air Balloon, only 2 miles from Birdlip, at Seven Springs and at The Reservoir Inn near Dowdeswell Reservoir on the A40.

* * *

Resume the route by taking the woodland track rising on the northern side of the road which descends Birdlip Hill. This track winds among trees and comes to a path junction. Bear left and go on to another path junction. Bear left for about 70 yards to the promontory viewpoint of The Peak, then backtrack to the junction and continue ahead (ignoring the path approaching from the right). Leave the woods and maintain direction along the left-hand edge of a field, then follow a switchback course along the scarp edge of Barrow Wake with broad panoramas to enjoy as you walk. There are two topographs here; one giving geological details, the other a topographic panorama. The path eventually winds up to road-level. Continue ahead alongside the road to reach The Air Balloon (Grid ref: 935161) *(Refreshments).*

Cross the road with great care to a gate. Through this bear left and follow waymarks among some trees, then walk beside a drystone wall as far as the promontory of Crickley Hill with its Iron Age hill fort (3). Bear right along the scarp edge to an observation platform, continue through the car park and by way of a wooden kissing gate into a meadow. Walk along the right-hand edge of the meadow and through a narrow strip of beechwoods. The waymarked path continues along the scarp edge to Shurdington Hill where you join Greenway Lane and turn right.

As you walk along Greenway Lane you can see the Devil's Chimney standing proud of the steep cut of the scarp half-left ahead. The route to it will double the actual crow-flying distance from this point.

Greenway Lane leads to the B4070. Cross and continue ahead on a minor road towards Ullenwood Manor (a training centre for the disabled). Beyond the manor's entrance the road curves to the right, you break away to the left on a track next to a golf course. In inclement weather the lower part of this track (a bridleway) can be exceedingly muddy and waterlogged. Follow the track uphill, alongside a plantation to reach a country lane (Hartley Lane). Turn left and walk downhill for perhaps 300 yards, keeping a lookout for a narrow path climbing among trees and shrubs on the right. (It is signposted.)

The path climbs above a quarry and along the scarp edge with fine views on the approach to Leckhampton Hill. Watch for a path on the left that goes downhill a short way to give a view onto the Devil's Chimney (2) (Grid ref: 946184).

Back on the main path continue over Leckhampton Hill, then along the scarp edge round Charlton Kings Common heading first east, then south-east among gorse bushes and hollows where ragstone has been quarried in the past. Lovely long views brighten the day. The path leads through a spinney and down an enclosed rectangular field, eventually coming onto a narrow road where you continue straight ahead (passing a windpump in the right-hand field) on to the Seven Springs staggered crossroads (1). (**Note:** should you be in need of liquid refreshment at this point, the Seven Springs Inn will be found a few paces down the A436 to the right.)

There now follows a choice of route. The first is shorter and more straightforward but is not recommended in heavy traffic. It crosses the A435 and continues up the A436 for almost exactly a mile until coming to a track leading through the field on the left. Should you decide to follow this road route please take the utmost care as there is no pavement and traffic can be very heavy.

Alternative (waymarked) route: At the crossroads go over the A435 to find a footpath by a shed. This leads to a track which gradually rises between fields and comes onto a narrow road. Half a mile after joining the lane break away left on a footpath, then among trees branch left across a field (skirting a small pond and going beneath power cables). Through a gate walk alongside another field, then on a track through Chatcombe Wood. A track leads along the right-hand edge of the wood then onto a drive which brings you to the A436. Cross the road to a gateway opposite to rejoin the road route from Seven Springs (Grid ref: 978180).

Walk ahead across the field and continue through the strip of Wistley Plantation, pass through a gate and make a descent of a steep hillside meadow heading half-right to the bottom corner. Go through another gate and a group of trees then slope down towards Old Dole Farm. On the way to it you will come to a waymark post where you bear right to find yet another gate leading into Lineover Wood. Draped on the scarp slope it is an ancient woodland first mentioned in documents of the 9th century.

The path through Lineover Wood is obvious and waymarked. It makes a steady traverse, comes out over a stile then descends along the boundary of a meadow to another stile and an enclosed path going down steeply beside a lower section of the wood. At the bottom of this path continue down to join the A40 almost opposite the tall grey building overlooking Dowdeswell Reservoir.

Bear left on the road and pass The Reservoir Inn *(Refreshments)*, then cut back on the right on a drive/service road leading to the reservoir. Cross a sluice and take the path ahead which climbs steeply beside Dowdeswell Estate Plantation. It is a strenuous climb, very slippery following wet weather, but eased in places by a series of wood-braced steps. At the top of the slope a stile takes you onto a narrow farm road beneath high voltage power cables, then over a second stile into a large field about 30 yards from some barns.

In the field cross half-right to the opposite hedgerow, then off to the right alongside it. Cross a narrow lane and continue ahead along the boundaries of two more fields to a second narrow lane. Maintain direction (roughly northward) along this lane with its row of pollarded beech trees, taking the first turning on the left along another quiet country lane - also lined with beech trees.

Coming to a woodland shaw on the right, leave the lane and walk alongside the trees with a large triangular meadow on your left until you come to another narrow lane. Bear right to pass through a gate and continue ahead on a rising track. A stile then leads left from the track onto a path which contours over a rough patch of hillside. Head to the right on a clear path among spiky bushes of gorse. Go through a wooden gate onto an enclosed section. The track opens and makes a lengthy traverse of the hillside, then goes along the lower edge of a beechwood. Pass through a wooden gate and, now on a path curving left, walk alongside a fence. At a path junction go ahead through another gateway and follow the path as it climbs (quite steeply in places) among clumps of hawthorn and brings you to a metal field gate leading onto Cleeve Common. (Note the transmitter masts half-right ahead, they will appear and disappear with annoying frequency over the ensuing miles. After a lengthy tour of Cleeve Common you will find yourself very close to them again - but having walked a 4 mile circuit!)

Wander ahead (slightly leftwards) to follow the scarp edge first to the earthworks of an Iron Age hill fort, then beyond this along what is known as Cleeve Cloud, with Castle Rock showing proud ahead. Coming level with Castle Rock (about a mile after having entered Cleeve Common), waymarks send you away from the scarp, heading to the right over the golf course to a trig point and topograph on the 1,040 foot summit. Short waymark posts lead the continuing route north-westwards, descending towards The Ring, above which you curve to the right.

The village of Cleeve Hill lies below, and those in need of overnight lodging or refreshment should break away here and cut down to the road (Grid ref: 984268) *(Accommodation, refreshments, shop).*

* * *

SECTION 10: CLEEVE HILL TO WINCHCOMBE

(See Map page 48)

Distance: $6^1/2$ miles.
Map: O.S. Landranger series; Sheet 163 (Cheltenham & Cirencester Area), 1:50,000.
Accommodation: Winchcombe - b&b.

The onward route continues the tour of Cleeve Common; a circuit that exploits a constantly changing series of panoramas - in good conditions that is. In inclement weather Cleeve Common wears a very different face and, when the mists are swirling, one needs to be able to use a map and compass. This high, exposed semi-moorland is the last of the region's unenclosed land and is designated a Grade 1 Site of Special Scientific Interest. In season a variety of orchids may be found here, together with a rich summer population of butterflies.

However, this is only one aspect of the walk. Elsewhere, away from Cleeve Common, there is an historic angle: Belas Knap is a splendid example of a Neolithic chambered tomb of the Severn-Cotswold Group, and the Way enters its wall enclosure in order to give an opportunity to study it. Then there's the site of a Roman villa, only about 100 yards off the path, and shortly before entering Winchcombe you catch sight of the 15th century Sudeley Castle.

From Cleeve Hill the Cotswold Way leads round the northern edge of Cleeve Common, then cuts south over the 'empty' hinterland before drawing away again through a vast, open agricultural landscape and entering the drystone walled compound of Belas Knap. Down then to Humblebee Woods, along a country lane, across the fields to Wadfield Farm and from there over more fields to Winchcombe. An interesting, varied walk but with no opportunities for refreshments along the way.

* * *

From The Ring (north-west of the trig point on Cleeve Common) waymark posts lead onto a golfers' track heading north-east towards the club-house. Before reaching the club-house, however, note the waymarks leading to the right to rise over the golf course. They eventually take you steeply down towards a woodland, with views beyond this into the Postlip Valley.

Near the wood a path veers slightly to the right and comes to a pond known as the Washpool (probably a sheep-dip). Beyond this the path enters a narrow, steep-sided cleave, and walking through its bed you will notice old gravel workings above. A waymark directs you out of the cleave with a stiff climb to the left. The ground eases and the path continues. There are many cross-tracks, but waymark posts lead you roughly south-east, then south, keeping well to the left of the transmitter towers. A track eventually takes you to a metal field gate and off Cleeve Common at last.

A clear track now heads almost due east through large open fields and brings you to a crossing track at Wontley Farm. Turn left and take the track rising ahead for a little over half a mile, then bear right through a gateway and follow a drystone wall ahead. This will bring you directly to Belas Knap Long Barrow (3) (Grid ref: 020254). This is certainly one of the most impressive sites along the Cotswold Way. An explanation panel gives details.

Cross the stile into the walled enclosure and, having given time to studying this impressive site, go out again by way of a kissing gate in the northern corner. Bear left and walk along the right-hand edge of the hilltop field, initially with woods beside you on the right.

At the bottom of the next field bear left to find another kissing gate which takes you into woods and down through them to a narrow country lane. Bear right and walk along the lane for about 400 yards (fine views off to the left) until you come to a track breaking away to the left, descending to Humblebee Cottages. On the way to the cottages note a clump of conifers enclosed by a wall standing in the field to the left. This marks the site of Wadfield Roman Villa (2) (Grid ref: 024260).

A track continues from Humblebee Cottages between more large fields to the handsome early 18th century Wadfield Farm. The route passes to the right of the farm buildings, then down the right-hand side of two sloping fields before passing through a gap on the right. Maintain direction, now with the hedgerow to your left. Cross a stream and a set of bars into the next field which you cross diagonally to the far corner. A stile in the hedge is crossed and you maintain direction over the field to another stile which leads to the last field on this stage of the walk. (Waymarking is exemplary over Wadfield Farm's land.) Halfway across this final field a telegraph pole bears a footpath sign. At the far side you come onto a narrow lane and bear left.

Coming across the fields from Humblebee Cottages there have been glimpses of Sudeley Castle (1) nestling in the valley among trees. On the road now you walk into Winchcombe, passing the castle's entrance on your right. Continue along the lane, which brings you into Winchcombe's main street by way of Vineyard Street near the Church of St Peter (Grid ref: 024282) *(Accommodation, refreshments, shops, post office).*

For information about Winchcombe, see details at the end of Section 2 of the South-bound Route.

* * *

SECTION 11: WINCHCOMBE TO STANTON

(See Map page 41)

Distance:	8 miles.
Map:	O.S. Landranger series; Sheet 150 (Worcester, The Malverns & Surrounding Area), 1:50,000.
Accommodation:	Stanway - b&b, camping. Stanton - b&b, camping.

Much of this stage wanders below the scarp face, although above Hailes Abbey the Cotswold Way climbs onto the wolden escarpment for a little under a mile before dropping down the slope again. This is a peaceful walk, a gentle lowland treasure of long views and tiny villages, of superb specimen trees and individual buildings here and there that make you pause and wonder.

The Way leads through Winchcombe and into a quiet farmland, across a former saltway and by the side of the ruins of Hailes Abbey (which had a 500-year chequered history and is worth a brief visit). From Hailes the route goes into orchard country and up to yet another hill fort site before coming onto an old drove road to Stumps Cross. Down then to Wood Stanway tucked against the hill and across the fields to the tiny village of Stanway with its Jacobean gatehouse, its 12th century church, its great tithe barn and lovely thatched cricket pavilion set upon staddle stones. The continuing path leads through the stately parkland of Stanway House, over a handful of low-lying fields and into one of the loveliest of all Cotswold villages, Stanton.

On this stage of the walk Stanton is the prime lure. It beckons unseen across the fields, and has the effect of elevating this to a truly memorable outing - even without the day's other attributes that in themselves ought not to be lightly dismissed.

* * *

Entering Winchcombe from Vineyard Street, turn right and walk through the town along the A46. On the northern outskirts the road swings right and then left to cross the River Isbourne. Soon after this you leave it to head to the right along Puck Pit Lane. At first metalled, Puck Pit Lane becomes an enclosed track, then a footpath. Coming to a stile cross over and on the far side of a field you will find a footbridge to the left of a shed. Heading north-east cross a series of undulating fields, linked by stiles or kissing gates and guided by waymarks, until you come to a track. Bear left and walk along the track, then go through a metal field gate and join a lane (Grid ref: 045298). Turn right and walk along Salter's Lane (part of an old saltway travelling from Droitwich to the Thames Valley) for about 60 yards.

Leave Salter's Lane by turning left on a short farm track and take the footpath ahead which leads to a country road next to the ruins of Hailes Abbey (3). (Some of the ruins can be seen over the boundary hedge.)

Turn right and walk along the road. When it forks, take the left branch straight ahead on a track rising between Hailes Wood and orchards. Soon after the wood ends a stile by a signpost directs you into the left-hand meadow. There is little to be seen of the footpath on the ground, but the Way leads diagonally up the slope towards a clump of trees, reached by way of a gate and a stile. The group of beeches marks the spot where it is said Thomas Cromwell overlooked the dismantling of Hailes Abbey. A hunting gate here gives access onto Beckbury Camp (2), another of the many Cotswold hill forts (Grid ref: 064299).

Turn left and walk along the field boundary with big views into the Vale of Evesham, then bear right at the far side, still along the left-hand margin of the field. Pass through a gap in the wall and resume direction towards a little woodland where you come onto a crossing track, a former sheep drove road. Bear left and walk along this track (called Campden Lane) for about half a mile, passing on the way a few farm buildings and a sorry-looking corrugated shed on staddle stones.

The track brings you to the B4077 at Stumps Cross (Grid ref: 076303). Do not go onto the road. Instead, pass through the gate towards it and immediately turn left round a wall, through another gate and follow the left-hand wall heading north-east to the lip of the escarpment at the end of a line of trees. Now descend the slope to pass well to the left of a house marked on the map as Lower Coscombe, then cross several fields linked by waymarked gates or stiles to a track by Glebe Farm. Passing the farm to your left continue down the track and onto a metalled road in the farming hamlet of Wood Stanway.

Turn right past Wood Stanway House, go through a gate and walk ahead along the left-hand boundaries of successive low-lying fields. You emerge onto the B4077 once more on the outskirts of Stanway (sometimes known as Church Stanway to avoid confusion with Wood Stanway). Go left for a few paces, then turn right to cross a small meadow and continue on a footpath alongside Stanway Estate

Tithe barn and church in Stanway

Yard. Beyond this you come to another narrow lane in the hamlet of Stanway (1). *(Accommodation).*

Bear right and follow the lane as it swings past the Jacobean gatehouse of Stanway House, then the church. Soon after this note, through the private gateway to Stanway House, a lovely old tithe barn on the right and in the meadow on the left an attractive thatched cricket pavilion set upon its staddle stones.

A stile on the right, found soon after passing the entrance to Stanway House, takes you into green parkland which you cross half-left among stately chestnut trees. Leave the parkland at its north-east corner by another stile and follow the continuing footpath over several fields, skirting the foot of the slope. A broad panorama lies ahead and to the left while the village of Stanton draws you on. You enter the village by a corrugated-iron Dutch barn where you bear left. On the road, head to the right (Grid ref: 068341) *(Accommodation, refreshments, shop).*

For information about Stanton, see details at the end of Section 1 of the South-bound Route.

* * *

SECTION 12: STANTON TO CHIPPING CAMPDEN
(See Map page 32)

Distance:	10 miles.
Maps:	O.S. Landranger series; Sheets 150 (Worcester, The Malverns & Surrounding Area) and 151 (Stratford-upon-Avon & Surrounding Area), 1:50,000.
Accommodation:	Broadway - hotels, b&b, camping. Chipping Campden - hotels, b&b.

The final stage of our long walk from Bath, this is something of an up and down course, perhaps a little strenuous on account of the height to be gained and lost, but full of variety and interest. There are some fine long views to draw the eye, easy tracks on the rim of the escarpment, the much lauded village of Broadway to explore, Broadway Tower to visit and, at the end of it all, glorious Chipping Campden to complete the pleasure of 102 miles of Cotswold wayfaring.

The splendours of Stanton lead directly to an uphill route where meadows and woodland clumps adorn the slopes of Shenberrow Hill. On the escarpment here yet another hill fort is to be found. Heading north along a track with a view the Vale of Evesham swallows distance far below. The Way then brings you down to woods and fields and into the crowded streets of Broadway. There's no peace to be had here, but the lovely buildings that line the wide main street hold your interest until it's time to climb again, this time to Broadway Tower. It is claimed that you can see 12 counties from the tower on a clear day, but attempting to put names to features in that vast panorama is likely to involve much argument and speculation. Better to remain ignorant and simply enjoy the view!

From Broadway Tower to The Fish Inn on Fish Hill is a green, undulating

undulating walk of little distance. Next follows a level stretch of arable farmland, then along The Mile Drive and onto Dover's Hill for the last big view of the walk before slipping innocently into Chipping Campden, a market town without equal and an elegant finish to an uplifting experience.

There are refreshments to be had in Broadway and at The Fish Inn on Fish Hill, about six miles from Stanton.

* * *

Stanton is so small a village that to walk straight through would occupy only a few short minutes, though to do so would be insensitive. This is a community to treasure, with streets to stroll along at an unhurried pace, cottages with roses over doorways to admire and the wolds rising behind, as if to offer protection.

So, amble down the street (Manorway) on entering, then swing sharp right where it forks to pass the old market cross. The street forks again and you bear right and wander past a delightful thatched cottage, soon to reach a gate leading to a track that rises out of the village. Keep on the track until, just before another gate, a waymark directs you to the right through a hunting gate by a pond (Stanton Reservoir). Work your way round and above the left-hand side of the reservoir, staying close to the right-hand boundary of a sloping meadow, and find a stile leading into the adjacent field. Resume direction, but now with the field boundary on your left, and come to a tight cleave among trees. (This can be rather muddy in inclement weather.)

Go up the cleave to Shenberrow Hill (6), bear left and pass through a field gate by a hill fort and follow the track ahead. This leads beside Long Hill Plantation on the scarp edge, then curves to the right to a cattle-grid. Bear left on a continuing track.

Views begin to extend out to the west as you wander along this escarpment track. It's easy walking, no route-finding problems, just the long views and cloudscapes with flowers at your feet and birds singing from the wayside scrub and crowns of trees.

The track then begins to lose height and comes to a cluster of farm buildings on the edge of Buckland Wood. Bear left now on a continuation of the track heading north for nearly half a mile. You approach a barn, which sits astride the county boundaries of Gloucestershire and Hereford and Worcester, and make a right-hand detour round it.

Having passed the barn on your left, resume direction and walk ahead along the right-hand boundary of a field. At the far side of the field you enter Broadway Coppice. Bear right and descend through this little woodland; when you emerge continue down the slope to a stile which takes you onto a narrow crossing lane at West End (Grid ref: 090371).

Cross the lane and continue directly ahead through fields linked by stiles. Cross over a footbridge and soon after this join a track leading into Church Street, almost opposite the Parish Church of St Michael's Broadway (5) *(Accommodation, refreshments, shops).* Turn left and wander down the street to the green, then bear right to walk through Broadway's busy High Street.

There's much to enjoy as you wander through, although the unrestrained commercialism tends to jar by comparison with Stanton, say. However, if it's refreshment you need, Broadway's the place. There are also shops in which to restock, if need be, for the remaining five or six miles of the walk.

Keep along the main street, passing the major junction of the Stratford road, and turning off to the right on a (signposted) farm track. Go through a gate, across a paddock to another gate, then bear half-left, pass through a gateway and continue uphill. The route soon follows a drystone wall all the way to Broadway Tower (4) (Grid ref: 114362).

Set upon a grassy knoll the tower enjoys a magnificent panorama, said to include 12 counties. It is now part of a country park, whose centre is found across the hilltop meadow to the south. The Cotswold Way, however, heads off to the left almost immediately, going through a gate and advancing across a rough undulating pasture, then veering slightly leftwards to a woodland. Enter the wood by a gate and follow the footpath winding through. It brings you out by the A44 at the top of Fish Hill, not far from The Fish Inn *(Refreshments)* (Grid ref: 119370).

Cross the road with due care and bear right to a picnic area with a topograph. A stile behind it leads into a field which you cross (entering Gloucestershire once more) to a country road. Go straight across the road and maintain direction over two more fields, then through a gap in a drystone wall to join The Mile Drive.

Wander ahead along The Mile Drive and at the far end enter a spinney by way of another gap in a drystone wall. The path brings you onto a country road where you bear right for about 400 yards or so, passing the Kiftsgate Stone(3) on the left which marks the site of an ancient meeting place. On coming to a minor crossroads turn left, soon after this you will come to a National Trust car park on the right giving access to Dover's Hill (2).

Walk ahead along the edge of the escarpment with lovely views into the Vale of Evesham to the left. When you reach a trig point bear right to find a stile. You now turn your back against the last extensive panorama of the walk, cross the stile and walk along the left-hand boundary of a field, emerging onto Kingcomb Lane (Grid ref: 144397).

Turn left and walk along the lane for about 100 yards, then head to the right on a descending track (Hoo Lane). This becomes metalled further down and leads to a junction by a thatched cottage. Continue ahead, then turn left by St Catherine's Roman Catholic Church into the High Street, Chipping Campden (1) *(Accommodation, refreshments, shops, post office etc.)*. Continue ahead, passing Sheep Street (on the right), then the Market Hall and many other lovely buildings, and turning right into Church Street. Walk the last few hundred yards to the Parish Church of St James, thus completing your 102 mile pilgrimage from Bath Abbey.

Shake the dust from your boots and be thankful for these days of exercise and beauty.

* * *

APPENDIX A: USEFUL ADDRESSES

The Cotswold Voluntary Warden Service,
c/o County Planning Department,
Gloucester County Council,
Shire Hall,
Gloucester. GL1 2TN.

The Ramblers' Association,
1-5 Wandsworth Road,
London. SW8 2LJ.

The Youth Hostels Association (England & Wales),
Trevelyan House,
St. Albans,
Herts. AL1 2DY.

Tourist Information Offices
Woolstaplers Hall Museum,
Chipping Campden,
Gloucestershire.

Cotswold Court,
The Green,
Broadway,
Gloucestershire.

Town Hall,
North Street,
Winchcombe,
Gloucestershire.

8 Abbey Churchyard,
Bath, Avon.

APPENDIX B: RECOMMENDED FURTHER READING

	Cotswolds - Leisure Guide (AA/Ordnance Survey 1986)
	The Cotswold Way Handbook (Ramblers' Association - bi-annual)
Brill, Edith	*Portrait of the Cotswolds* (Hale 1971)
	Life and Tradition in the Cotswolds (Dent 1973)
Crosher, G.R.	*Along the Cotswold Ways* (Cassell 1976)
Finberg, H.P.R.	*The Gloucestershire Landscape* (Hodder & Stoughton 1975)
Hadfield, C. & A.M.	*The Cotswolds: A New Study* (David & Charles 1967)
Hill, S.	*Spirit of the Cotswolds* (MIchael Joseph 1988)
Lewis, J.	*Walking the Cotswold Way* (David & Charles 1986)
Pevsner, N.	*The Buildings of England: Worcestershire* (Penguin 1968)
Richards, M.	*The Cotswold Way* (Thornhill Press 1982)
	The Cotswold Way (Penguin 1984)
Sale, R.	*A Guide to the Cotswold Way* (Constable 1980)
	A Visitor's Guide to the Cotswolds (Moorland Publishing 1982)
Smith, B.	*The Cotswolds* (Batsford 1976)
Verey, D.	*The Buildings of England: Gloucestershire, The Cotswolds* (Penguin 1979)
	Cotswold Churches (Batsford 1976)

Printed by CARNMOR PRINT & DESIGN
95-97 LONDON ROAD, PRESTON, LANCASHIRE, UK.